D1187094

UTOPIAN FANTASY

A Study
of English Utopian Fiction since
the End of the Nineteenth Century

by

RICHARD GERBER

ROUTLEDGE & KEGAN PAUL LTD.
Broadway House, Carter Lane
London

First published in 1955
by Routledge and Kegan Paul Limited
68 Carter Lane London EC4
and Printed in Great Britain
by Billing and Sons Limited
Guildford and London

To
Margarethe

' "*You speak of the city which has its being in words; for there is no spot on earth, I imagine, where it exists.*"

' "*No*", *I said;* "*but perhaps it is laid up in heaven as a pattern for him who wills to see, and seeing, to found a city in himself. Whether it exists anywhere or ever will exist, is no matter.*" '

Plato, 'Republic', ix, 592

CONTENTS

PREFATORY NOTE

I would like to express my gratitude to the British Council and to the Zürich Educational Council, whose joint support enabled me to work on this book as a Research Student at Queens' College, Cambridge, from 1950 to 1952; also to Mr. L. J. Potts and Mr. G. Hough, of Cambridge, with whom I had occasion to discuss my work. My thanks are due again to my wife, for her pains in typing the manuscript, and to Dr. J. C. Middleton and Mr. H. Weiss, for theirs in correcting the proofs. Finally I wish to express my gratitude to the *Jubiläumsspende* of the University of Zurich, for a grant without which the publication of this work would have been impossible.

INTRODUCTION

ALTHOUGH utopian fiction is an old form of literature it was not systematically studied before the end of the nineteenth century, when utopias were again recognized as a social influence. Then political economists began to write histories of utopian literature which were collections of summaries and criticisms of the utopian proposals of reform.[1] Later on sociologists and philosophers went beyond such reformatory details and started defining the principles of utopian thought.[2] The utopian's mental attitude became established as one of the most important forces in political reality, but simultaneously the literary fiction receded into the background. It is true that certain important utopias came in for individual literary criticism, but only lately utopian fiction has been recognized and studied as a proper literary genre, above all in V. Dupont's monumental history of English utopian literature.[3]

M. Dupont first lists all the reformatory details, then he considers the literary devices of all the utopias available. Thus his work is an indispensable reference book for the specialist. In M. Dupont's view utopias are skilful descriptions of ideal societies meant to be taken as practical contributions to social reform. The utopian writer is an active social reformer producing constructive political propaganda; therefore such imaginary voyages as *Gulliver's Travels* or *Erewhon* are not taken into account. Thus M. Dupont's work is restricted to a special kind of utopian writing up to 1914.

The present study has another aim. It is not concerned with the practical details of social planning, and only superficially with special literary devices. Above all it tries to show that the several characteristics of utopian literature are the outcome of a comprehensive utopian imagination and view of life. If we want to know what this imaginative force is we cannot set out with hard and fast definitions and typologies. Therefore not only socially constructive utopias are considered, but also various other kinds of imaginary commonwealths and fantastical countries. As a result utopianism often appears somewhat different from what it must be in a study based on 'classical' utopias only. Other differences arise because the material of the present study is modern: it is mainly taken from the twentieth century. The last fifty years or so have produced a surprisingly great number of utopian forecasts. Dupont deals only with five twentieth century products, and other critics hardly ever try to penetrate beyond the work of Wells, Huxley, and Orwell. A glance at the list of recent forecasts (Appendix) will give some idea of the far wider range and the popular force of modern utopian fantasy. Another glance at the same list will show that a great many of these products are subliterary. Because of their great number and their frequent mediocrity, and because this study aims to delineate the essentials of modern utopian fantasy in English fiction, these utopias are not considered individually, but thematically.

The first part of the study outlines the rise of the basic modern utopian attitude: the quasi-religious belief in the miraculous power of unlimited evolutionary progress. This comparatively recent development gives birth to new kinds of fiction. Then, in the second part, when tested by the social realities of contemporary civilization, this basic utopianism becomes more moderate and realistic and produces sociological forecasts in fictional form. The last part traces the growth of an adequate literary genre of fantastic fiction which enables the utopian to attain the closest possible connection with present-day reality and the reader's mind. Although widely differing as regards the problems of theme and method, these aspects are related to the same type of imagination and can be regarded as stages in the logical evolution of modern utopianism.

No attempt has been made to define a specifically English or Anglo-Saxon type of utopian imagination. Compared with continental utopias English utopian literature certainly has its minor national peculiarities, but in the main it expresses the hopes, fears, and dreams of all western civilization.

Part One

THE EVOLUTIONARY SETTING

I

THE RISE OF UTOPIAN HUMANISM

In the course of the last four centuries the use of the word 'utopia' has been so widely extended that it is very often difficult to establish a connection between the original meaning of the word and its derivatives. This development has been favoured by the inherent ambiguity of the term, which from the very start denoted a non-existent country on the one hand and a perfect commonwealth on the other. While the full title of More's work '*De optimo rei publicae statu deque nova insula Utopia libellus*' suggests that the two meanings are kept separate, the attached eulogistic poem symbolizes the essentially ambiguous character of the book in the pun:

> 'Wherefore not Utopie, but rather rightely
> My name is Eutopie.'[4]

This 'Eutopie' recalls all the old dreams of a perfect world, of a golden age, of a time and place where things are better and misery has no existence. During the Middle Ages these myths received support from Christianity in the idea of the Millennium, the Kingdom of Heaven on Earth. The Golden Age, the Millennium, and Utopia, all of them point in the same direction: the dream of a state where happiness will reign; Eutopia, Paradise.

But these different manifestations are linked to each other by more than a vague common desire for happiness; they are further related to each other by a common belief that this state of happiness is to be attained and realized on earth. The Golden Age, the Millennium, and Utopia are all different aspects of the *Earthly* Paradise. The Earthly Paradise was a real myth; it was conceived to be something quite different from the ordinary world and yet part of this world. Sometimes it was an island beyond the seas, sometimes a land situated underground, sometimes a country in the mountains; but wherever it was supposed to be, it was believed to be actually there and was traceable on mediaeval maps.[5] Men went in search of it: imaginary travellers like Mandeville wrote about it:

> 'And a iii journeys fro that see ben grete mountaynes, out of the whiche goth a great flood that cometh out of Paradys.'[6]

Even explorers like Columbus firmly believed in it:

> 'I think also that the water I have described may proceed from it [the Earthly Paradise], though it be far off, and that stopping at the place I have just left, it forms this lake. There are great indications of this being the terrestrial paradise, for its site coincides with the opinion of the holy and wise theologians I have mentioned.'[7]

The Earthly Paradise was a myth that fitted into a more primitive world-picture than ours; it was not consciously invented, but imagination and belief coincided in it. For in primitive man's ideas about the cosmos 'the line between the barely conceivable and the flatly impossible has not yet been drawn with any sharpness'.[8] Although utopia is also supposed to be realized on earth, it is very different from the myth of an Earthly Paradise in its imaginative character, which is new and modern. In the creation of Utopia man imposes his will on the imagination, and the non-existent ideal country loses its mythical force and becomes a device, a construct, a fiction. Spontaneous imagination and traditional belief are replaced by the fictive activity of logical thought.

> 'By fictive activity in logical thought is to be understood the production and use of logical methods, which, with the help of accessory concepts—where the improbability of any corresponding objective is fairly obvious—seek to attain the objects of thought. Instead of remaining content with the material given, the logical function introduces these hybrid and ambiguous thought-structures, in order with their help to attain its purposes indirectly, if the material which it encounters resists a direct procedure.'[9]

There are innumerable degrees of subtlety in the use of such fictive methods, and one of the subtlest and most ingenious means is provided by the utopian fiction, in which the existence of the ideal country is not meant to be taken literally, but as a help in discovering another, hidden level of reality that could not otherwise be perceived. This utopian fiction is developed from the earliest somewhat primitive sketches into the most sophisticated utopian novels in recent times.

With its conscious, often playful fictitiousness and its moral purpose being clearly perceptible in the presentation of an ideal country, the utopian fiction conforms closely to the most important requirements of the humanistic approach to art and literature. The humanist 'poet' is not so much an imitator; but, according to Sir Philip Sidney, rather the creator of 'another Nature', devoting his energies to 'the divine consideration of what may be, and should be'. Utopia is not only the result of a new social consciousness, but also the proper outcome of the humanist theories of literature applied to society in general. As such it is bound to be highly praised in Sidney's *Apology*:

> 'But even in the most excellent determination of goodness, what philosopher's counsel can so readily direct a prince, as the feigned Cyrus in Xenophon, or a virtuous man in all fortunes, as Aeneas in Virgil; or a whole Commonwealth, as the way of Sir Thomas More's Utopia? I say the way, because where Sir Thomas More erred, it was the fault of the man and not of the poet, for that way of patterning a Commonwealth was most absolute, though he perchance hath not so absolutely performed it.'[10]

This utopian fictive activity was rife in Greek times, but most of its products have been lost.[11] In spite of many earlier attempts, Sir Thomas More was the first significant writer to transform the non-existent ideal country from an object of naive mythical belief into the instrument of sophisticated rationalistic hypothesis. The naïve mind sees a possible reality as actually existing; its working seems to be perceptive and passive. The sophisticated utopian writer on the other hand is clearly aware of the gap between possible and actual reality, but tries to close it by giving to a possibility the appearance of actual reality: he is consciously creative and active.

Humanistic activity is not confined to the fictive creation of the happy country; it is also at work in shaping a different way of achieving happiness within this ideal country. In the one case happiness is a state of grace, in the other it is the result of a conscious human effort. The mythical Earthly Paradise is simply there, it has only to be found. One may even stumble on it, and then all problems will be solved: the happy man will live in a state of perpetual bliss where every effort is superfluous. As Treyer has pointed out, the same is true of the Millennium; it is not achieved, it comes, and no man can prevent or accelerate its coming; it will come when the proper moment arrives.[12] In both cases there is a sudden break in the chain of events and natural laws, the happy state is entered by a magical transformation or miracle. Things simply happen to man and the conditions undergo changes which human power cannot achieve:

> 'A place there is diffusing rivers four,
> With flowers ambrosial decked; where jewelled turf,
> Where fragrant herbs abound that never fade.
> The fairest garden in this world of God.
> There fruit knows naught of season, but the year,
> There ever blossoms earth's eternal spring; . . .
> In sun's hot rays it burneth not, by blasts
> Is never shaken, nor doth whirlwind rage
> With fierce-conspiring gales; no ice can quell,
> No hailstorm strike, nor under hoary frost
> Grow white the fields.'[13]

Utopian happiness is quite different in origin. The Utopians are happy because more and more efficient work is done. In one of the first passages of the second book the Utopians astonish the outside world by digging a big canal by organized effort. The Utopians were educated to be a better people by their king, who applied his intelligence to the organization of society, replacing mere chance and arbitrariness by constructive thought. So the social as well as the temporal or spatial reality of Utopian society are constructs.

There are further differences connected with these two states of earthly happiness. The transitions from the ordinary world to the Earthly Paradise and the Millennium are essentially journeys out of time. In the Earthly Paradise time comes to a stop. The fountain of youth arrests progress in time, and when Bran returns from the Land of Youth he dissolves into ashes, for, having lived outside time, it is impossible for him to come back.[14] Similarly the Millennium is the first stage on the way to eternity; both the Earthly Paradise and the Millennium are lower, sensuous aspects of Heaven, which is completely outside time. In comparison with the absolute bliss awaiting man outside time, the existence in time must be considered miserable and sinful, and the way out of time is the only satisfactory solution. The Earthly Paradise, the Millennium, and Heaven are different aspects of a religious vision, in which man is found to be rooted in a power that lies beyond ordinary experience. In such a view time can be conceived as a horizontal line, leading nowhere in particular, while miracles, visions, mystical unions, and death are the immense verticals transcending time and reaching out towards eternity.

In a utopia on the other hand the accent is set on man in this world; the utopian is not primarily religious, but humanistic. In the early utopias, such as More's and Bacon's, the stress on man in this world does not lead to an anti-religious attitude, for man is still seen as surrounded by religion wherever he goes and whatever his actions may be. But all the same, the religious and the utopian view cannot be entirely reconciled: if this life is essentially sinful and imperfect, what is the good of bettering conditions? Is it not a futile endeavour? In More's and Bacon's case, their active temperaments break down the restrictions imposed by this essentially paralysing belief. Their spontaneous concern with man in this world and their insistence on what he may achieve sometimes become so strong that the religious background recedes. More's Utopians adopt a natural religion that at times cannot be very easily distinguished from a worldly hedonistic philosophy:

> 'Therefore even very nature (saye they) prescribeth to us a joyful lyfe, that is to say, pleasure as the ende of all oure operations. And they define vertue to be lyfe ordered accordynge to the prescripte of nature.'[15]

In spite of the Utopian hedonistic calculus, bodily pleasures are not overrated. Moreover More's religious conscience interpolates a critical comment in Hythloday's remarks, whose attitude is more determined by the orthodox religious view:

> 'But the chiefe and principall question is in what thinge, be it one or moe, the felicitye of man consistethe. But in this poynte they seme almooste to muche geven and enclyned to the opinion of them, which defende pleasures, wherein they determine either all or the chiefyste parte of mans felicite to reste.'[16]

More's attitude is tempered by reason; one should alleviate conditions as much as possible, since it is not good to forget and neglect earthly things although Heaven will come. But Heaven is more important, and man is not proud in *Utopia*; in fact pride is considered the most evil vice.

The typically modern Proud Man is found for the first time in Bacon's *New Atlantis*. A religious foundation is laid at the beginning, but is almost completely forgotten later on. The most important building, Solomon's House, is not a church, but a research institute, 'the noblest foundation (as we think) that ever was upon the earth, and the lantern of this kingdom'.[17] Although 'it is dedicated to the study of the works and creatures of God',[18] this devotional aspect recedes when Bacon begins to deal with the inventions and treasures of this institute. While in Utopia the priest is the only person who is magnificently dressed, in New Atlantis the member of Solomon's House proceeds in splendour and triumph, which gives occasion to an orgy of elaborate description of the riches surrounding Man, the Master. This member 'had an aspect as if he pitied men'.[19] 'He held up his bare hand as he went, as blessing the people, but in silence.'[20] The greatest jewel he can give to his visitors is the knowledge of the state of Solomon's House. He imparts it to them in a long power-drunk speech in which he enumerates the large number of marvellous inventions in their possession.

> 'The end of our foundation is the knowledge of causes and secret motions of things, and the enlarging of the bounds of human empire, to the effecting of all things possible.'[21]

But in spite of this optimism the notion of a glorious future is not yet fully expressed, as the dominant notion of time was not favourable to such an expression. There is no real vision of infinite progress, since time is still limited by religious beliefs, some of them even predicting that the world was nearing its end. Although there is no reason to suspect that Bacon was affected by this particular idea, there is proof that he was influenced by biblical chronology when working out the historical frame for *New Atlantis*. According to Bacon Atlantis disappeared some 3,000 years ago, quite in contradiction to Plato's account, in which this event was placed 8,000 years earlier. But the Platonic hypothesis might have contradicted the more important biblical authority.[22]

The idea of progress and human perfectibility does exist in these early utopias, but since it is not supported by an adequate world-picture, it is not more than a seed. The progressive attitude only becomes really powerful and realistic with the emergence of a new view which sees progress not only as a moral postulate, but as a historical reality derived from an observation of facts. Then time expands into an endless vista, not confined by a closely dated beginning and an abrupt ending, nor dwarfed by verticals leading out of it into eternity.

Such an adequate background for utopian humanism was provided by the theory of evolution. Here, by ceasing to be separate entities and by becoming interdependent, men are no longer static, nor time empty. Everything is seen as an infinite evolutionary growth and flow, in which the anticipation of a glorious future for mankind on earth replaces transcendental happiness in a timeless God. Man becomes truly humanistic and self-reliant, and even transcendental religion has to be adapted to his practical purposes:

> 'We may prophesy that as the evolutionary concept of ethics spreads, organized Christianity will devote less attention to salvation and the life hereafter, more attention to realization of the Kingdom of God on earth.'[23]
> 'The religious impulse, itself one of the social forces to be more fully comprehended and controlled, will increasingly find its outlet in the promotion of the ideals of the Socialized State.'[24]

So religion is reduced to a psychological impulse, a social force which has to be and can be directed in accordance with the ends of man, which in their turn are created by man himself. 'Purposes in life are made, not found.'[25] For humanistic activism it is not enough to believe that evolution is automatically progressive because some benevolent anonymous life-force is at work. Man has to be shaping his destiny quite independently, although encouraged by the proved possibility of progress. The creed of 'scientific humanism' may also be called the creed of utopian humanism because of its long, far-reaching vista.

> 'Humanism, with the aid of the picture given by science, *can* achieve a framework strong enough for support. In the light of evolution it can see an unlimited possibility as a continuation of the long process of biological betterment that went before the appearance of man. If humanism cannot have the fixed certitude of dogma, it can at least have an attitude of direction and aim. The altruistic forces of human nature need not be restricted to isolated acts of doing good. They can harness themselves for the task, inspiring because of its very size, of slowly moving mankind along the upward evolutionary path.'[26]

The last metaphor, the upward evolutionary path, is significant for the change which has taken place. Time and history can no longer be pictured as a horizontal line with vertical connections to Heaven, while man is being pulled about by contradictory forces. Now he is seen as climbing the purposeful, infinitely ascending resultant of the two previous vectors. Time has become dynamic.

'At last we have an optimistic instead of a pessimistic theory of this world and our life upon it. Admittedly the optimism cannot be facile. . . . Perhaps we had better call it a melioristic rather than an optimistic view; but at least it preaches hope and inspires to action.'[27]

This is a fairly sober statement of the belief giving support to the utopian writers. In its light an exhortation to change society, or even to change human nature, is no longer an empty phrase to which the obvious reply was: You cannot do it, human nature is human nature and will always remain the same.

The theory of evolution affects not only the plausibility of utopian optimism, but the very character of utopian planning:

'The Utopia of a modern dreamer must needs differ in one fundamental aspect from the Nowheres and Utopias men planned before Darwin quickened the thought of the world. Those were perfect and static states, a balance of happiness won for ever against the forces of unrest and disorder that inhere in things. . . . Change and development were dammed back by invincible dams for ever. But the Modern Utopia must not be static but kinetic, must shape not as a permanent state but as a hopeful stage, leading to a long ascent of stages. Nowadays we do not resist and overcome the great stream of things, but rather float upon it.'[28]

Although indulging in rather too easy an optimism in his last few words, Wells is right when attacking one of the radical weaknesses of earlier utopias. The evolutionary conception of a modern utopia does away with that 'ineradicable illogicality' which Treyer perceives in all utopian constructions:

'Here we touch the limit of utopian thinking which cannot be crossed; we touch as it were its ineradicable illogicality. Some historical process has to and is to lead into utopia. But no historical process—this is the postulate—is to lead out of it and beyond it. Utopia must be without history. It fights *against history*, and this fight must be lost.'[29]

This judgment on utopian writing and thinking is a hasty generalization based on conclusions drawn from some 'classical' utopias. Picturing the history of utopias as a slow decadence and disintegration since the days of Plato, Treyer is unable to see that the different modern philosophical and scientific background gives new depth and strength to more recent utopias, enabling them to surmount just those difficulties which Treyer describes as unsurmountable.

The evolutionary upward path ceases to be a mere background when the writer tries to imagine this progress in greater detail. Julian Huxley states the general principles, but refrains from drawing a concrete picture, nor is he drunk with his vision, describing the glorious future in a lyrical outburst. But once the concept of evolutionary progress is accepted, extreme enthusiasm proceeding from deep conviction becomes possible. Utopia ceases to be a mere logical construct, a mere persuasive device. After passing from myth to fiction, the idea of the Earthly Paradise assumes once more the nature of a genuine myth where 'the line between the barely conceivable and the flatly impossible' cannot be drawn at all. Sometimes the future has such tremendous proportions that every attempt at visualizing it is bound to fail:

> 'What grandeur of life may not open out to Man! Eye hath not seen, nor ear heard; nor hath it entered into the mind of man to conceive. . . . For now we see as in a glass darkly. . . .'[30]

Others are more definite. The earliest and most typical post-evolutionary utopian outburst is contained in Winwood Reade's *Martyrdom of Man* (1872). His fantastic assumptions, which have hardly been surpassed by more recent utopian visionaries, appear all the more fantastic because the astonishing developments seem to come about quite effortlessly and naturally. But once his original assumption, the idea of endless progressive evolution, has been granted, why should the details be questioned?

> 'These bodies which we now wear belong to the lower animals; our minds have already outgrown them; already we look upon them with contempt. A time will come when science will transform them by means which we cannot conjecture, and which, even if explained to us, we could not now understand, just as the savage cannot understand electricity, magnetism, or steam. Disease will be extirpated; the causes of decay will be removed; immortality will be invented. And then, the earth being small, mankind will migrate into space, and will cross the airless Saharas which separate planet from planet and sun from sun. The earth will become a Holy Land which will be visited by pilgrims from all quarters of the universe. Finally, men will master the forces of Nature; they will become themselves architects of systems, manufacturers of worlds. Man then will be perfect.'[31]

The seed planted in Bacon's House of Solomon has grown rapidly in the hothouse of progressive evolution.

Progress, evolution, transformation are words which sound encouraging as regards mankind in the abstract; but what satisfaction does the individual derive from these grand visions? How do they help him? When seen from the level of such a glorious future does he not appear to be just as miserable and pitiable a being as he appears in the eyes of the angels? And how is he to be comforted for his loss of individual spiritual significance?

> 'Famine, pestilence, and war are no longer essential for the advancement of the human race. But a season of mental anguish is at hand, and through this we must pass in order that our posterity may rise. The soul must be sacrificed; the hope of immortality must die. A sweet and charming illusion must be taken from the human race, as youth and beauty vanish never to return.'[32]

Individual significance has to be preserved by a change of religion; instead of being linked to some extratemporal, eternal reality the individual is linked to mankind in time. If time were conceived to be an empty and meaningless abstraction, this would mean a loss of significance for the individual. But since the march of time is identified with progress, the impression is created that the individual is still linked to some final significant reality, although in rather an indirect and roundabout way. In the final analysis this new concept of a significant reality may be called Life.

> 'The only significance we can see attaching to man's place in nature is that he is willy-nilly engaged in a gigantic evolutionary experiment by which life may attain to new levels of achievement and experience.'[33]

Nor is man's dignity jeopardized by such a conception, he is not seen as just one form of life among many others of equal value. On the contrary man has to shoulder a tremendous responsibility, for he alone is the highest and most valuable product which has been created by the evolutionary process so far.

> 'Only along one single line is progress and its future possibility being continued, the line of man. If man were wiped out, it is in the highest degree improbable that the step to conceptual thought would again be taken, even by his nearest kin.'[34]

So man is finally at the highest point of all nature, reigning supreme with no authority above him.

> 'Scientific humanism is a protest against supernaturalism: the human spirit, now in its individual, now in its corporate aspects, is the source of all values and the highest reality we know.'[35]

Such is the view which gives the fullest meaning and the widest scope to progressive utopianism, and almost exactly the same view animates the work of the most important representative of twentieth century utopian writing, H. G. Wells. Since valuable life is of the greatest importance, and since mankind represents the highest value in life as a reality as well as a possibility, the fullest satisfaction for the individual is to be found in submerging himself in this greater whole which is a new deity with a different name.

> 'We work, we think, we dispute, we take risks and suffer—for there seems no end to the difficult and dangerous adventures individual men and women may attempt; and more and more plain does it become to us that it is not our own little selves, but Man the Undying who achieves these things through us.'[36]

This is the attitude of a future, utopian generation in Wells's *Shape of Things to Come*. The satisfaction felt in this religious participation in Man the Undying derives from a feeling of delegated pride and power, which was first expressed in utopian writing in Bacon's *New Atlantis*. But now the world is no longer even nominally to be inquired into as the cleverly executed work of God, but exists for man to do with as he likes. Each man is a member of a supreme élite merely by being a man, even though his claim for being considered a human being may be a purely biological one.

The stress on evolutionary utopian progress is to a great extent biological, for this seems to be the most proper, radical and efficient way for man to gain greater power, and more and more various life. Greater intellectual and moral insight may come with evolutionary progress. The evolutionary quest is less for an ideal man making the best of present possibilities than for a superman whose intellectual and moral superiority is founded on his superior biological development. On this ground the argument that the belief in evolutionary progress is no more than a wild goose chase, can be effectively countered:

> 'Finally, it appears to me that his [Aldous Huxley's] denial of validity and importance to any notion of progress in time,

> especially on the ground that its goal is an ever receding one, cannot be maintained, and indeed is illogical, even if we were to agree that unitive knowledge of the Divine Reality were the only pure or final end of man. For there was a stage in the temporal history of our earth, a very long stage, extending for over a thousand million years, when the attainment of unitive knowledge by living creatures was impossible, for want of the physical machinery of body and nervous tissue with which to attain it.'[37]

So the straightest road to progress and the extinction of evil seems to be the physical development of man.

> 'With a few more cubic inches of brain for the average man and a score of years added to the span of life . . . every present difficulty in the human outlook would vanish like a dream.'[38]

This idea has been imaginatively used in more than one modern utopia. A fairly clear idea of the nature of such a future superman who will be so different from us is of some importance, for the truth of his image will determine our feelings about the reality of evolutionary progress. The whole religion of progress is based on some process of identification, but what identification is possible between us, the primitive men, and the future supermen who may prove to be beings of another, strange species?

> 'Here is the essential question: What sort of human beings will be alive in days to come? We can only be interested in them if their life will have value and dignity of a kind which has continuity with the human existence we have known for millenniums in the past. Our descendants must be such as can recognize us as their forefathers, not necessarily in the physical or in the historical sense.'[39]

2

MAN AND SUPERMAN

WHAT sort of human beings will be alive in days to come? This is the vital question which the writers of evolutionary utopias are trying to answer. Julian Huxley contents himself with generalities like 'the upward path of man', Winwood Reade gave a more definite, but still very sketchy picture. In utopian fiction there has to be further concreteness, the writer cannot leave the question as it is, but, by giving substance to a mere speculative possibility, he has to convert it into an imaginative reality. His statements are, however, not meant to be taken as accurate predictions, but only as indicators of one possible development among many, or of some essential development where the minor details do not matter.

> 'We are not to set up as historians attempting to look ahead instead of backwards. We can only select a certain thread out of the tangle of many equally valid possibilities. But we must select with a purpose.'[40]

The conception of such a definite future may seem quite plausible to the reader, or even highly probable, and it will carry the conviction or a true myth, with religious significance.

> 'But when we once realize the periods of time which our thought can and should envisage we shall come to see that the use, however haltingly, of our imaginations upon the possibilities of the future is a valuable spiritual exercise.
>
> 'For one of the essential elements of religion is an emotional attitude towards the universe as a whole. As we come to realize the tiny scale, both temporal and spatial, of the older mythologies, and the unimaginable vastness of the possibilities of time and space we must attempt to conjecture what purposes may be developed in the universe that we are beginning to apprehend.'[41]

The literary possibilities in this field have been sketched by Shaw, who calls *Back to Methuselah* 'my beginning of a Bible for Creative Evolution',[42] and then goes on:

> 'It is my hope that a hundred apter and more elegant parables by younger hands will soon leave mine as far behind as the religious pictures of the fifteenth century left behind the first attempts of the early Christians at iconography.'[43]

Several attempts have been made since then, the most ambitious and significant in the field of fiction being Olaf Stapledon's *Last and First Men*, which achieved sufficient popularity to be published as a Pelican Book.

> 'Yet our aim is not merely to create aesthetically admirable fiction. We must achieve neither mere history, nor mere fiction, but myth. A true myth is one which, within the universe of a certain culture (living or dead), expresses richly, and often perhaps tragically, the highest aspirations possible within that culture. A false myth is one which either violently transgresses the limits of credibility set by its own cultural matrix, or expresses aspirations less developed than those of its culture's best vision. This book can no more claim to be true myth than true prophecy. But it is an essay in myth creation.'[44]

Success in such an attempt is very difficult indeed, for the obstacles to be surmounted by all utopian writers are great, and in many ways even more so in the case of what may be called 'evolutionary utopias', in contrast with the utopias of social reconstruction. The evolutionary time range is longer, and the writer is therefore nearer the realm of the purely fantastic and runs the danger of indulging in absurd speculations and of lapsing into amusing nonsense. But the writer can show that he has to be fantastic in order to be realistic in such a case:

> 'Had I chosen matter in which there was nothing whatever of the fantastic, its very plausibility would have rendered it unplausible. For one thing at least is almost certain of the future, namely, that very much of it will be such as we should call incredible.'[45]

But even a writer like Stapledon, who is almost crazily fantastic at certain times, agrees that this cannot be the main vehicle for carrying conviction:

'if such imaginative construction of possible futures is to be at all potent, our imagination must be strictly disciplined. . . . The merely fantastic has only minor power.'[46]

The supermen should not only be superhuman, but also human. In utopian writing it is therefore very often hard to say where man ends and the superman begins, but on the whole we can make a rough distinction between the utopian ideal man and the evolutionary superman. The utopian ideal man is such as we could be if only we had not been hindered in our natural development by the trammelling old-fashioned institutions of an outworn society. In Wells's *Modern Utopia* we meet the utopian ideal man, the better self, or our 'Utopian self', as Wells calls him. In such a utopia

'We must assume there is a man such as I might have been, better informed, better employed, thinner and more active.'[47]

And when the narrator actually makes his utopian self's acquaintance, this is what he sees:

'He is a little taller than I, younger looking and sounder looking; he has missed an illusion or so, and there is no scar over his eye. His training has been subtly finer than mine; he has made himself a better face than mine.'[48]

This is not a meeting between man and superman, the aim envisaged being definitely practical and attainable within the course of the next hundred years or so. Perhaps it is even going too far to call this particular utopian self an ideal man; one might rather be inclined to describe him as a man living under 'ideal' conditions.

The imaginary people in Wells's later utopian book, *Men Like Gods*, are a stage further removed from reality. They not only go naked, or nearly so, but the spectators' reactions are also of a totally different order.

'He had never seen so beautiful a face and body before.'[49]
' "What a perfect form!" he said. "I admit I was wrong," said Mr. Burleigh with deliberation. . . . "These are no earthly people".'[50]

These 'easy-mannered brown-skinned divinities' live longer than ordinary men; they look forty when they are over seventy and they have achieved direct thought-transmission without interference by the spoken word. The last makes them definitely supermen, although some precaution has to be used as regards this fact. In this instance thought-transmission is rather an incidental feature, created by the requirements of the story much more than by the need of a lifelike and imposing picture of supermen.

Both people, the Modern Utopians and the Godlike Men, are still men living under ideal conditions; they are quite naturally felt to be men and members of the same species, and in all such cases no effort is needed to relate them to our conception of humanity, for they are immediately recognized as our better selves, even if we do not exactly agree with the author's opinion on the nature of the recommended reforms. In accordance with the near kinship of the ideal men and ourselves the time range of such works is strictly limited, so that the evolutionary forces have no room for strongly influencing man's physical and psychical constitution. *Modern Utopia* is placed in a spatially removed co-present, and the world of *Men Like Gods* is only three thousand years older than ours.

The increasing space allowed to fantasy with the extension of the time range is well exemplified by the different stages of Shaw's *Back to Methuselah.* There the presentation becomes more difficult once the limit of the next few hundred years has been reached and crossed, and the relation between man and superman becomes a rather tenuous one. This strangeness is also the strength of such pictures, since their supermen are more interesting than the rather sentimentally sweet descriptions of Apollonian godlike men. Moreover the antagonism between man and superman provides ample material for a thrilling conflict between opposite forces.

Bulwer-Lytton's *The Coming Race*, published in 1871, provides a typical early instance of an evolutionary utopia and of the uses to which this form can be put. It may be considered the starting point for the modern development of utopian fiction. It does not merely set forth a race of supermen, but it is saturated with the evolutionary concept. It is much more evolutionary than *Erewhon*, which, apart from the *Book of the Machines*, does not show much evidence of the influence exerted by evolutionary thought. Moreover, even the *Book of the Machines* is only concerned with discussing the possibility of a new emergence and not with realizing in concrete detail the result of such a possible growth. The Coming Race, the Vril-ya, are in looks more or less like ordinary human beings, but taller, about seven feet high, and they are much more powerful, since their thumbs are longer, their palms proportionately thicker, and since a visible nerve runs from the wrist to the tips of their fore- and middle-fingers. These special features enable them to handle the mysterious force called Vril. By using this strange natural source they can kill at almost any distance, they can hypnotize people, they can destroy anything they want to, in short, with its help they can do almost anything man can think of. The acquisition of this power, which bears some faint resemblance to electricity or subatomic energy, has taken place in the course of the last seven thousand years. The Vril-ya are also strikingly handsome, although their complexion tends to be somewhat strangely coloured. Above all, they have attained to an almost complete inward peace which strangely illuminates their features:

> 'The beauty of their countenances is not only in symmetry of feature, but in a smoothness of surface, which continues without line or wrinkle to the extreme of old age, and a serene sweetness of expression, combined with that majesty which seems to come from consciousness of power and the freedom of all terror, physical or moral.'[51]

They are truly supermen and constitute an ideal which cannot possibly be achieved by ordinary men within the next few generations. Because the gap between them and ordinary man is so great, a conflict arises in the very first encounter between the intruder from the surface world and the representative of the Vril-ya. This encounter symbolically represents man's instinctive reaction before the evolutionary idea has been completely absorbed and turned into a new religion. The ordinary man involuntarily shies away from the superman, and is by no means comforted by the thought that he is a link in the historical chain of which the superman is another part.

> 'But the face! it was that which inspired my awe and my terror. It was the face of man, but yet of a type of man distinct from our known extant races. The nearest approach to it in outline and expression is the face of a sculptured sphinx—so regular in its calm, intellectual, mysterious beauty.
>
> 'The face was beardless; but a nameless something in the aspect, tranquil though the expression, and beauteous though the features, roused that instinct of danger which the sight of a tiger or a serpent arouses. I felt that this manlike image was endowed with forces inimical to man.'[52]

This feeling of being threatened by the emergent supermen is not lost all through the book, in spite of all his admiration for them. Whenever the hero comes into contact with them he realizes that he is not fit to live among them and cannot be happy in a world of supermen. This feeling is intensified in the course of the book and expresses itself in violent action; for instance, when one of the supermen sheds his wings which the visitor had taken to be part of his body:

> 'That sudden transformation did but increase my horror, and as extreme fright often shows itself by extreme daring, I sprang at his throat like a wild beast.'[53]

This conflict is not confined to single outbursts. In time it becomes the main driving force for the progress and conclusion of the story. The action is not any longer accidental as in More's early sketch of a narrative, where Hythloday simply returns to Europe for no cogent reason. Mentally the underground visitor manages to adapt himself well enough to the Vril-ya conditions, but physically he becomes the unfortunate victim of his underdeveloped constitution. The women are taller than the men in this race and they love things which they can pet. Physical passion is not very important at this stage of the evolution of man. So this small and miserable specimen of mankind makes a good object for women's liking for pets. Finally one of the superwomen even wants to marry the visitor. This would involve the deterioration of the subterranean race. Therefore the visitor is to be killed. But before the innocent victim can be exterminated, he is saved and brought back to earth by the loving woman.

Romance, satire on women's rights, evolutionary theories, thrilling action, and other ingredients are inextricably mixed, as in so many other cases. But the main theme that spurs the story onward at an ever increasing pace consists in the instinctive reaction of man who refuses to be transcended. *The Coming Race* is an evolutionary utopia, but antiprogressive in spirit. In order to make his antiprogressive point, the author keeps stressing the danger produced by modern man's desire to transcend himself, for, according to Bulwer-Lytton, he would lose the qualities that are essential to him, if he did so.

Bulwer-Lytton's supermen are only one kind among many in modern utopian stories. In other cases these supermen achieve great spiritual powers, and telepathy is a constant element;[54] some of them can walk on the waters or even hover in the air without any mechanical help;[55] most of them develop their mental capacities beyond any limits set to present man and depend less and less on outward conditions such as food, clothing, and temperature, etc., etc. There is no need to study all or even a large proportion of these fantastic creations or to enquire into degrees of scientific plausibility.

Evolution explains anything and everything if only the time range is long enough. Even in the earliest utopias without supermen there are historical accounts describing the evolution of society which has led to the utopian state, although evolution may seem rather too modern and pretentious a term when applied to such historical thumb nail sketches as the following:

> 'Utopus, which also broughte the rude and wild people to that excellent perfection in al good fassions, humanitye, and civile gentilnes, wherin they nowe goe beyond al the people of the world.'[56]

or

> 'Their cronicles, whiche they kepe written with all deligente circumspection, conteinynge the historie of M.vii.C.lx. yeares, even from the firste conquest of the Ilande, recorde and witnesse that the houses in the beginning were very low, and like homely cotages or poore sheppard houses, made at all adventures of everye rude pece of tymber that came firste to hande, with mudde walles, and ridged roofes, thatched over with strawe. But nowe the houses be curiouslye buylded after a gorgious and gallante sorte, with three storyes one over another.'[57]

A much longer historical flash-back is inserted in Bacon's *New Atlantis*, but here the stress is less on the evolution and development of a new society than on the course of natural history with its series of earthquakes and inundations which have shaped the earth into its present form. All this had been done before in a very similar way by Plato when accounting for the disappearance of Atlantis in *Critias* and *Timaeus*. Bacon is merely imitating his Greek model and changing a few details. Since then the imaginary history and the imaginary evolutionary account have become more and more important. Theoretically it might seem as if the utopian writer could content himself with relying on the force of the catchword 'evolution' to explain everything. But using the evolutionary concept in such a general, abstract way would not be very different in character from employing magic in order to account for strange and improbable occurrences. Using the mere scientific term is not enough; the picture has to be filled in with more detailed imaginative strokes in order to become even superficially plausible; the reader's attention has to be cleverly directed along a possible historical and evolutionary path.

Historical and evolutionary accounts are very prominent in *The Coming Race*, which may again serve as a typical illustration.

Several phenomena have to be accounted for in this case: the existence of an underground race, their superhumanity, and their perfectly working organization, which is not simply the result of their superhuman moral qualities. The origin of such an underground race is supposed to have been brought about by huge prehistoric inundations which forced the people to take refuge in caverns, where they were gradually lost in the interior of the earth. All this is imagined as a very slow geological process, quite different from the biblical picture of Noah's Flood. Even the Vril-ya notions about these happenings are uncertain and mythical, since they occurred so long ago. Then the historical stages set in. At first the state of the underground society resembled very much our own till it was brought to an end 'by the gradual discovery of the latent powers stored in the all-permeating fluid which they denominated Vril.'[58] The use of this mysterious fluid is intimately connected with the biological evolution of man, since it depends on the development of a specific nerve in the hand:

> 'It has been slowly developed in the course of generations, commencing in the early achievements and increasing with the continous exercise, of the vril power; therefore, in the course of one or two thousand years, such a nerve may possibly be engendered in those higher beings of your race, who devote themselves to that paramount science through which is attained command over all the subtler forces of nature permeated by vril.'[59]

The development of vril power necessitates an evolution of society, for the indiscriminate, individual, almost anarchical use of this immensely effective power within the old-fashioned framework of society threatens to destroy mankind altogether. So the organization of society and the rules guiding the conduct of men are changed for the better by sheer force of circumstance. Existing within this new peaceful society man's spiritual and mental nature is also changed; a process which can be accurately traced in a big Vril-ya picture gallery:

> 'The type of face began to evince a marked change about a thousand years after the vril revolution, becoming then, with each generation, more serene, and in that serenity more terribly distinct from the faces of labouring and sinful men.'[60]

The biological evolution of man, the development of vril power, the change of society, and the emergence of a new mentality all go together and cannot be separated from each other. The whole evolutionary process is summarized and satirized in a chapter where a Giant Frog represents the great-grandfather of a Prometheuslike philosopher and where the relative values of man and frog are sophistically discussed in an absurdly serious way which is meant to be a parody on some of the more extravagant evolutionary controversies.

The ideas treated in this story are not very original, nor is the use made of them brilliant; but both, ideas and technique, are a typical illustration of the general method employed by modern utopias: they forecast the picture of a very slow, but steady development in a certain direction.

> 'In the beginning of the twentieth century you could not see the ground for clever men. . . . And all these clever men were at work giving accounts of what would happen in the next age, all quite clear, all quite keen-sighted and ruthless, and all quite different.'[61]
> 'But the way the prophets of the twentieth century went to work was this. They took something or other that was certainly going on in their time, and then said that it would go on more and more until something extraordinary happened.'[62]

Several circumstances prevent *The Coming Race* from being an evolutionary fantasy proper. *The Coming Race* as well as the great majority of the utopias from More to Orwell conform to the same established relation between the utopian past and present: there is the utopian fixed time, e.g. 1984 or 674 A.F. on the one hand, and the occasional historical flash-backs on the other. The main narrative line can be pictured as a horizontal in a utopian present which is intersected by vertical excursions into the past.

Where the evolutionary idea is more important than the exact description of an imaginary society, the story is of a different order. Occasionally the utopian present may then be seen as suspended between the real present and a far future which can only be perceived as through a haze.[63] Or the main narrative line is a vertical with several horizontal excursions on different time planes. Historical foreshortening and abstraction are thereby prevented. This is essentially the technique of the time-traveller who can arrest his progress whenever he likes, as in Wells's *Time Machine*. There we are shown successive pictures of the present, the future and the far future. This technique of presenting tableaux of different evolutionary stages has been used again and again with more or less ingenuity in many not so well-known works. We are, for instance, introduced to some prehistoric ideal civilization. Then we race through history and the present. Thousands of years later, we get acquainted with an over-organized and equalized society which lives partly underground, fearing future wars in the air. Thousands of years later again men live completely underground, digging deeper and deeper, almost antlike in their organization. At long last, thousands of years later again, man and ant merge into each other.[64] This is the 'go-ahead' technique with a vengeance.

In all these evolutionary fantasies with different time sections a complete inversion of the ordinary utopian narrative method has taken place. In most of the well-known utopias the adventures in utopia are the frame for one or more historical accounts, but here the time journey, the rapid historical account, becomes the frame for a varying number of adventures in utopias on different time levels. Although such a narrative technique is much nearer to the evolutionary concept, it is not quite adequate to the idea of the evolutionary flow. It presents a series of interludes, of separate acts, as in Shaw's *Back to Methuselah.* For the stage this is certainly the only possible way of presenting evolution, but not for fiction, which can create a continuous imaginary historical and evolutionary account. In spite of that the presentation of different subsequent time sections remains popular. Olaf Stapledon's *Last and First Men* is probably the only fully developed evolutionary utopia, and it is by far the most ambitious and sustained attempt to create an 'evolutionary bible'. It sums up the problems treated in this chapter and points to some essential formal problems of the imaginary history.

This summary history of mankind during the next few million years traces the rise and decline of eighteen different races of men. All through this development Stapledon is very much concerned with one of the main tasks confronting the writer of utopias: the connection between present and future humanity. Stapledon improves considerably on the pure straightforward evolutionary technique, which would lead him in a straight line to some extreme. The fantastic eighteenth species, the very apex of humanity, has been achieved by a long story of trial and error. A kind of spiral evolution takes place, consciously guided by human effort. It works slowly upward in continual struggle of thesis, antithesis, synthesis, until the marvellous eighteenth men arise. This continuous testing of man's re-creation by man gives direction and interest to the story, but in the early undirected evolutionary parts the way of achieving plausibility has not noticeably changed since *The Coming Race,* although the terms employed have a more scientific ring:

> 'An incursion of the sea gradually isolated some of their number on an island continent, which was once part of the North Atlantic Ocean-bed. The climate of this island gradually cooled from subtropical to temperate and sub-arctic. The vast change of conditions caused in the imprisoned race a subtle chemical re-arrangement of the germplasm, such that there ensued an epidemic of biological variation. Many new types appeared, but in the long run one, more vigorous and better adopted than the rest, crowded out all competitors and slowly consolidated itself as a new species, the Third Men.'[65]

This is a rather summary procedure and after repeated easy handling of thousands and millions of years the imaginative effort required exhausts the reader. He loses any time-sense left and sees the more or less fantastic creations succeeding each other as if there were hardly any interval to separate them, especially since Stapledon's book keeps accelerating the succession by covering ever longer time ranges in the different chapters. In the end millions of years seem like so many minutes or even seconds—an effect aimed at in order to give the impression of the extremely small importance attaching to our own restricted existence. Nevertheless, the method becomes tiresome and less and less plausible with every further step, although the extreme of absurdity is reached very early in the book, in the scientifically constructed Fourth Men. These 'Great Brains' are huge super-brains lodged in large cement towers, artificially fed and cultivated. Being inhuman they are doomed to extinction, and the 18th Men are much more nearly related to present man. They are an ideal which should possibly inspire humanity:

> 'He [present man] would consider them sturdy, often thick-set folk, but he would be compelled to allow them grace of movement and even beauty of proportion. The longer he stayed with them the more beauty he would see in them, and the less complacently would he regard his own type.'[66]

So the connection between the last and first men is established in an emotional and imaginative as well as in an evolutionary way. These supermen live for thousands of years, they have attained telepathy, they can explore the past with their minds in a way that cannot even be explained. They also achieve 'group consciousness' in sexual groups consisting of ninety-six subsexes, at certain times even 'race-consciousness', a communal racial ecstasy comprising all the many millions of Neptune men. Their telescopic eye at the top of their heads allows them to observe the stars more clearly, and their space-ships communicate with the planets. They could even move Neptune, if they liked; for mentality, the highest value in humanity, can achieve almost anything.

With its enormous time range and its numerous evolutionary changes which explore most of the regions of biological fantasy, Stapledon's book reaches the limits of the evolutionary account. In spite of its immense vista and a great deal of original thought which makes this imaginary history not so absurd as it might sound, it cannot be called a literary success. The ever recurring themes, the migration to Venus and later to Neptune, make for a certain monotony. This tendency is increased by the inherent dryness of the style. The grandiosity of the time vision and the fantastic evolution is quite lost in a pedestrian rendering which makes everything seem to be simple, almost commonplace. Therefore many things which might be mysteriously puzzling and haunting become meaningless and absurd. Partly this is also the result of Stapledon's lack of space. He keeps rushing through the developments, so that certain phenomena are dealt with on one page which would require a whole book in order to convey some sense of their reality and possible beauty. Given the huge quantity of material which this evolutionary fantasy deals with, it cannot be artistically successful and is therefore likely to remain the only attempt in this direction. Other attempts would have to be greatly condensed and reduced to a clearer and simpler pattern.

The dry scientific description of strange beings seems to be adequate in cases of strange queer horrors such as the lunar men in Wells's *First Men in the Moon*. Where the supermen are meant to be inspiring ideals, a dreamlike haziness seems to be more effective, suggesting rather than plainly stating the possible developments. So the supermen in J. D. Beresford's *What Dreams May Come* or in E. Meredith's *Our Stranger* are much more convincing, just because they are not so clearly and plainly pictured. Without any poetic suggestiveness which could give meaning to terms like 'group-consciousness', etc., such evolutionary accounts are doomed to remain fantastic science fiction. Since the long range evolutionary account does not leave enough room for this, it defeats the aim of utopian writing, which is the achievement of ever greater imaginative reality.

3

THE PROBLEM OF SURVIVAL

MANY of the supermen in utopian fiction embody one of the oldest dreams of man: the dream of man's immortality. Generally it is a dream whose realization depends upon transference into another world. But for the utopian this dream has to come true here on earth, or at least in some physical form in space. 'Immortality will be invented', as Winwood Reade thought.[67] Some writers would object to such a use of the term and distinguish between immortality and survival.

> 'Immortality is participation in the eternal now of the divine Ground; survival is persistence in one of the forms of time.'[68]

The writer of evolutionary fantasies is concerned with survival, the survival of man, the fittest and highest form attained by life. For evolutionary progress and the survival of mankind, individual immortality is by no means necessary, but may even be a hindrance. But in the very far future the superman may be conceived as immortal, and therefore godlike, or as godlike, and therefore immortal. Individual immortality is one of the attributes of the perfect superman, and extremely long individual life is a characteristic feature of all the utopian dreams covering a greater time-span. They all tend to go 'Back to Methuselah'. In part this is simply due to an innate desire to keep alive and avoid death. This desire must be even stronger in a utopia, for here the individual only finds the rather dry and abstract satisfaction of living on in mankind, while in the religious view he may attain to a personal afterlife. In all the utopias that are supported by a more or less orthodox religious view, extreme length of life is not aimed at and death is calmly faced, as in More's *Utopia* or in Bulwer-Lytton's *The Coming Race*. In a materialistic and purely hedonistic society like that of Aldous Huxley's *Brave New World* this stoical calmness has to be produced by early death-conditioning. But as early as *New Atlantis* there is an attempt to secure longer life:

> 'We use them [caves] also sometimes (which may seem strange) for curing of some diseases, and for prolongation of life in some hermits that choose to live there, well accommodated of all things necessary, and, indeed, live very long;'
> 'And amongst them we have a water which we call "water of paradise", being by that we do to it made very sovereign for health and prolongation of life.'[69]

A very modest and innocent elixir of life, compared with some of the later ones. But very soon long life and near-immortality are achieved by other means, sometimes by a purely evolutionary process.[70]

The mere prolongation of life would be pointless if there were no progress achieved. Most of these 'Back to Methuselah' romances therefore combine longer life with a correspondingly deeper insight into the nature of things. A typical example of this tendency is *Back to Methuselah* itself. The works of Wells and Stapledon express the same ideas. Longer life secures a higher mentality, and both together assure for the individual a wealth and variety of experiences that in our world can only be experienced by the group. So the superman becomes godlike, not just by being immortal like a god, but by participating in all the various aspects of life till he can see it as steadily and wholly as a god. In all such cases long life is the equivalent of a long vigorous youth, even if it is sometimes subtly disguised as in *Back to Methuselah.* There, in spite of their aged appearance, in their minds the wise men are youthfully alert.

It is here that these imaginings of long life are open to attack. Long life and old age accompanied by loss of mental and bodily vigour are identified by the opponents of such utopian desires. In their creations Tithonus-like creatures go on living, gradually declining into senescent idiocy. Such are Swift's Struldbrugs. In *After Many a Summer* Aldous Huxley similarly stresses the survival of mere animal vitality while the mental and spiritual capacities are reduced to nothing.[71]

In Stapledon's *Last and First Men* the Last Men consciously refuse to become immortal. Not only is individual immortality more fantastic, but it does not even seem wholly desirable. It may be said that an individual cannot imagine his own death, but it seems at least as hard, if not harder, to imagine oneself living on forever here on earth. The utopian therefore wants to save the individual not from death but from a sense of futility and frustration. His task is eminently one of giving man's short life significance within a greater framework. As we have seen, this is done by considering each individual as an active participator in the long evolutionary struggle.

This progress opens an apparently infinite vista. Man has been evolved during the last few million years. The evolution of man will go on and on, higher and higher. This seems to be satisfaction enough. But will it go on and on? How can it go on and on? These are questions which the exercise of evolutionary speculation must raise sooner or later. By placing man's destiny in time only, the evolutionary utopian has set up an aim, a far-away ideal, but at the same time he threatens mankind and all it stands for with complete extinction. For one thing seems certain:

> 'The star on which we live had a beginning and will doubtless have an end.'[72]

To the utopian mind it does not matter when exactly this end will come. It may not come for millions and millions of years, but if it finally does come the whole struggle for progress and the superman must appear meaningless. This problem is raised by the earthly visitor, Barnstaple, in Wells's *Men Like Gods*:

> 'It has been a belief in our world that at last there must be an end to life because our sun and planets are cooling and there seems no hope of escape from the little world upon which we have arisen. We were born with it and we must die with it. That robbed many of us of hope and energy: for why should we work for progress in a world that must freeze and die?'[73]

The answer in this case is a simple reassertion of utopian optimism. But a vague existential anxiety is hardly ever wholly absent in such books; sometimes this shows itself in the fact that such optimistic assertions are far too positive and consequently assume a certain stridency. In all such cases time is no longer the friend assisting man on his infinite upward path; it is the deadly enemy.

> 'But at my back I always hear
> Time's winged chariot hurrying near.'

This general anxiety has found its expression in several fantasies of the future, Wells's *Time Machine* being the best-known of them. Having seen humanity at some date in the far future, the time traveller journeys on till all life on our planet has vanished and a feeling of deadly desolation and fear overcomes him:

> 'The showering white flakes in the air increased in number. From the edge of the sea came a ripple and a whisper. Beyond these

lifeless sounds the world was silent. Silent? It would be hard to convey the stillness of it. All the sounds of man, the bleating of sheep, the cries of birds, the hum of insects, the stir that makes the background of our lives—all that was over. As the darkness thickened, the eddying flakes grew more abundant, dancing before my eyes; and the cold of the air more intense. At last, one by one, swiftly, one after the other, the white peaks of the distant hills vanished into blackness. The breeze rose to a moaning wind. I saw the black central shadow of the eclipse sweeping towards me. In another moment the pale stars alone were visible. All else was rayless obscurity. The sky was absolutely black.'[74]

In *The Time Machine* we see the world long after mankind has disappeared from the surface of the earth. In other nightmarish visions of the future we may see the last representatives of mankind engaged in the struggle against an inexorable fate, slowly or rapidly defeated by the inimical forces of nature.[75] The same fate of ultimate extinction overcomes Stapledon's Last Men, although they arrive at a certain heroic grandeur by stoically accepting it:

'In the vast music of existence the actual theme of mankind now ceases for ever. Finished, the long reiterations of man's history; defeated, the whole proud enterprise of his maturity. The stored experience of many mankinds must sink into oblivion, and to-day's wisdom must vanish.'[76]

A certain satisfaction arises from their inclination to see the history of mankind as an immense existential symphony where every theme is necessary although the meaning of the whole eludes man's grasp. Nevertheless the predominant note is one of despair rather than one of religious acceptance. Even the Samurai in Wells's *Modern Utopia* are frightened of 'The Night of this World'.

'The time when our sun will be red and dull, and air and water will lie frozen together in a common snowfield where now the forests of the tropics are steaming.'[77]

But very soon utopian optimism reasserts itself:

'I remember that one night I sat up and told the stars very earnestly how they should not escape us in the end.'[78]

These nightmares are overcome by sheer optimism, which is mostly strongly supported by arguments relying on the use of utopian superscience. It is generally conceded that the earth will end sooner or later, but there are other planets, even other stellar systems. In our age of interplanetary societies such projects and speculations can hardly any longer be called utopian. Fictional accounts of such interplanetary journeys are very numerous; their quality is generally of a low order, the main interest being provided by crude 'scientific' sensationalism. There are not so many specimens of the more thoughtful variety, telling us how man colonizes other planets in order to escape his impending doom. Stapledon's *Last and First Men* and J. B. S. Haldane's *Last Judgment*[79] both try to perform the role of optimistically supporting scientific myths. In both cases mankind at first does not seem to be able to realize the danger. The majority remains quite unmoved and sadly unutopian. Then an intelligent and courageous minority recognizes the responsibility placed on them:

> 'A few hundred thousand of the human race, from some of whom we are descended, determined that though men died, man should live forever.'[80]

After an immense loss of human life Venus is finally colonized; Stapledon's future men go on to colonize Neptune, after long adaptations of human physiology to new conditions. There mankind is wiped out by an accident. But in Haldane's truly optimistic utopian view the prospect is unlimited. Jupiter will be colonized and from there, in the course of time, other stellar systems may be reached after the circumstances have undergone a favourable change. C. S. Lewis's *Out of the Silent Planet* satirizes this frantic attempt in the person of Weston, the scientist struggling for mankind's survival. Weston is the first representative of those few hundred thousand men who have decided that man must go on for ever and take the risk of interplanetary journeys in order to achieve that end. Weston, Devine, and the reluctant Ransom travel to Malacandra (Mars). There Ransom tries to explain Weston's motives to Oyarsa, the spiritual ruler of Malacandra, in simple Malacandrian language:

> 'I think he would destroy all your people to make room for our people; and then he would do the same to other worlds again. He wants our race to live for always, I think, and he hopes they will leap from world to world . . . always going to a new sun when an old dies . . . or something like that.'
> 'Is he wounded in his brain?'[81]

Weston's own words are spoken in the grand utopian style:

> 'It is in her [Life's] right,' said Weston, 'the right, or if you will, the might of Life herself, that I am prepared without flinching to plant the flag of man on the soil of Malacandra: to march on, step by step, superseding, where necessary, the lower forms of life that we find, claiming planet after planet, system after system, till our posterity—whatever strange form and yet unguessed mentality they have assumed—dwell in the universe wherever the universe is habitable.'[82]

This might seem a very obvious and violently distorted parody of the utopian view, but it reflects almost word for word the opinions and hopes expressed in such speculative accounts of the future as Haldane's *Last Judgment*. There the announcer on Venus proclaims:

> 'Our galaxy has a probable life of at least eighty million million years. Before that time has elapsed it is our ideal that all the matter in it available for life should be within the power of the heirs of the species whose original home has just been destroyed. If that ideal is even approximately fulfilled, the end of the world which we have just witnessed was an episode of entirely negligible importance. And there are other galaxies.'[83]

The future life of mankind seems to be secured beyond all doubt, although in a very roundabout and sometimes even precarious way. It is significant that, in Haldane's words, all the matter available should come within the 'power' of man. Apart from felicity, power has been one of the main drives in utopian dreams since the days of Bacon, power over nature in all its forms. Therefore it is only natural that in a forecast of a state where the power drive is more apparent, such a rather roundabout way of securing survival should be regarded as highly unsatisfactory. In Orwell's *1984* power over death is achieved in a much more radical way by a new application of 'solipsism': 'reality control'. Here the evolutionary wheel has come full circle, and evolution itself is abolished. At the beginning of the development man was seen to be part of God's timeless reality. Later on the utopian derives his satisfaction from the progress and evolution of proud mankind. But then the dangers and uncertainties of the march of time become evident. So evolution is abolished, the state of immortal superhumanity is declared achieved in the present, through reality control by the Party.

> 'You will learn by degrees, Winston. There is nothing that we could not do. Invisibility, levitation—anything. I could float off

this floor like a soap bubble if I wish to. I do not wish to, because the Party does not wish it. You must get rid of those nineteenth century ideas about the laws of Nature. We make the laws of Nature.'[84]

Man is the only reality:

'Before man there was nothing. After man, if he could come to an end, there would be nothing. Outside man there is nothing.'[85]

This 'collective solipsism' enables the party to gain ever greater power. Winston, the old evolutionary heretic, thinks that Life will defeat them. The answer is:

'We control life, Winston, at all its levels.'[86]

The Party also controls death, for although individual life may be shortened more and more, it does not matter in the least, for the collective organism will go on living for ever:

'Can you not understand that the death of the individual is not death? The Party is immortal.'[87]

The same argument that comforts the evolutionist comforts the party member, only the feeling of belonging to an élite has been further accentuated. Not all the crude forms of human life can be called humanity:

'Humanity is the Party. The others are outside—irrelevant.'[88]

Here the existential anxiety at work in the evolutionary utopias has led to collective paranoia.

But this anxiety may take other shapes in the utopian imagination; sometimes mankind is supposed to be threatened by other forces than the march of time. Although man thinks of himself as the highest and most valuable manifestation of life, dominating all other creatures, from time to time he is assailed by strong misgivings. In Swift's utopian satire, doubt of human superiority was based on moral grounds. There degenerated man is dominated by the wise horses. But these Houyhnhnms are only allegorical creatures, symbolizing the eighteenth century equation of reason and nature. In the evolutionary fantasies such imaginings cease to be playful. The modern utopian may be really haunted by the fear that he might be superseded in the evolutionary struggle by other forms of life. Then he desperately starts fighting in his imagination against the Martians and all similar non-human invaders who are very often superior to man in their intelligence and achievements. If they are really superior, man ought to acknowledge defeat, but here the evolutionary concept breaks down.

> 'The forces that evolved us in the long succession of living beings endowed us with a tenacity of self-assertion that rebels against the bare idea of giving place to rats or unclean intrusive monsters equipped with streptococci for our undoing.'[89]

The survival of the fittest cannot be accepted if one's own race is extinguished in the process. Moreover, there is an instinctive feeling at work that mankind, in spite of all its shortcomings, is essentially superior to other forms of life; and this feeling persists in the face of actual proof that the other beings have attained deeper insight. But then, mankind might evolve even higher representatives of life in the far future. Whatever the exact line of reasoning may be, the sense of the human values at stake gives deeper meaning to such sensational tales as Wells's *War of the Worlds*. Scientific warfare on a large scale does not form the most significant aspect of the book. It is not simply a war like any other war, only infinitely more sensational and catastrophic. The most salient feature consists in the danger to mankind, its imminent extinction, and its incredible degradation when crushed by another form of life. As in the *Time Machine* the atmosphere pervading *The War of the Worlds* is one of doom. This is not merely a playful speculation, for if the hope of mankind's survival seems real to the utopian, the danger of being conquered by beings from other planets must seem equally real.

> 'It was the beginning of the rout of civilization, of the massacre of mankind.'[90]

In order to humble proud man even further, to reach the extreme of utopian masochism, man is imagined to be mere cattle, serving as living food for the Martians.

> 'They [the Martians] did not eat, much less digest. Instead, they took the fresh living blood of other creatures, and *injected* it into their own veins. . . . Let it suffice, blood obtained from a still living animal, in most cases from a human being, was run directly by means of a little pipette into the recipient canal. . . .'[91]

Such a procedure must seem highly implausible, even to the layman who does not know much about blood groups. But nevertheless a nauseating thrill is achieved, a glance into utopian hell. In the old Christian world-picture, mankind knew two extremes: the saint and the inveterate sinner. One was destined for Heaven, the other for Hell. In the evolutionary world picture and its corresponding myths, godlike blissful existence is assured to the superman who proves victorious in the evolutionary struggle, extinction or cruel slavery devours the subman who does not possess the required qualities. The two aspects may be visualized by the same writer, as in Wells's works. They may even be pictured in the same book, e.g. in Orwell's *1984*. Here one part of mankind has to become subhuman in order that the other part may be superhuman. The argument runs: A superman dominates everybody else. If I dominate everybody else, I am the superman. How can I be sure that I dominate everybody else? By inflicting pain, for inflicting pain on somebody proves to me that he is in my power. Therefore, the more pain I can inflict the more superhuman I become. *1984* is rich in short cuts to superhumanity.

It is not only the minds of speculative utopians that are haunted by the spectre of the war with another dominant species; even the mind of the man in the street is affected by such imaginings. Some striking proof for this was furnished by the widespread panic in the U.S.A. on the 30th of October 1938, when Orson Welles broadcast an adapted version of the *War of the Worlds*. Hundreds of thousands were gripped by a wild fear, convinced that the end of mankind was at hand.[92] That incident not only showed that a great number of people thought an invasion from Mars quite credible, that the utopian interplanetary mythology is eminently alive; but it also made people realize the value of Human Life. Suddenly every aspect of human civilization appeared attractive, and it seemed sad, even tragic that all this was going to be destroyed. Even in the wildest panic many people kept thinking of mankind as a whole, a proof that the evolutionary racial concern is not merely theoretical. Even a young student frantically racing away from the supposed place of catastrophe found time to consider the greater issues:

> 'I thought the whole human race was going to be wiped out—that seemed more important than the fact that we were going to die. It seemed awful that everything that had been worked on for years was going to be lost forever.'[93]

The threat to humanity by other beings has proved to be a popular theme, not only in English fiction. Sometimes such tales are merely sensational, sometimes satirical as in Karel Capek's *War with the Newts*. In other cases such a common danger may be used in order to give a sense of unity to quarrelling mankind; and therefore the threatening supercrabs in a book like Eden Phillpotts's *The Owl of Athene* must be considered a beneficent force. Such an outside danger spurring mankind on to a concerted effort can also take the shape of earthquakes, huge meteors, whirlwinds, etc.[94] There are always new variations on the theme, but whatever the variation may be, in all cases where mankind is threatened by other beings, the essentially superior value of mankind is postulated. Where man cannot prove victorious, he tries at least to prevent his enemy from taking his place. So in Stapledon's *Last and First Men* humanity will stoically accept its own death, if the destruction of the strange radioactive Martian clouds is assured by this sacrifice.

In all these tales the elements of fantasy and inhuman horror play an important part. The greater the horrors of the appearance and mentality of the strange visitors, the clearer the desirability of all that is human appears in comparison, and the greater the sensational thrill achieved. In order to secure these combined effects such creatures are generally so designed that they seem superior in power and mechanical intelligence, but infinitely inferior, disgusting, and repulsive in all the aesthetic and moral aspects. In C. S. Lewis's *Out of the Silent Planet* Ransom sums up all the salient features of this technique of extra-terrestrial horror when he hears that he is to be given up to the 'sorns' on Malacandra:

> 'He had read his H. G. Wells and others. His universe was peopled with horrors such as ancient and medieval mythology could hardly rival. No insect-like, vermiculate or crustacean Abominable, no twitching feelers, rasping wings, slimy coils, curling tentacles, no monstrous union of superhuman intelligence and insatiable cruelty seemed to him anything but likely in an alien world. . . .
> 'The "sorns" would be . . . would be . . . he dared not think what the "sorns" would be. And he was to be given to them. . . . He saw in imagination various incompatible monstrosities—bulbous eyes, grinning jaws, horns, stings, mandibles. Loathing of insects, loathing of snakes, loathing of things that squashed and squelched, all played their horrible symphonies over his nerves. But the reality would be worse: it would be an extra-terrestrial Otherness—something one had never thought of; never could have thought of.'[95]

This extract not only shows the traditional horrors of the extra-terrestrial journey, but also illustrates the fact that a recent writer, working in an established tradition, can achieve a new kind of horrible thrill. He can rely on the reader's memory and create an anticipatory dread which even surpasses the fear evoked by the actual presence of the strange beings. The change of mood, the feeling of relief are all the greater, when the reality turns out to be better than was expected. Ransom mentions H. G. Wells, and most of his anticipations seem to be based on his recollections of the Martians in *The War of the Worlds*, which must be regarded as the very peak of the horror-technique of actually presenting such creatures in every detail. They glisten like wet leather and their oily skin seems somehow fungoid; their immense eyes are extraordinarily intense; their V-shaped mouths quiver incessantly and saliva drops from their lipless brims. Their bodies heave and pulsate convulsively and they possess a large Gorgon group of tentacles, etc., etc. All this creates a nauseating dread in the spectator and may exert a certain hypnotic fascination on many readers. Although the thrills of such romances are built on different foundations, such tales can be considered as the most effective modern equivalents of the old Tales of Terror.

In the utopian imagination, mankind can be wiped out by time, natural forces, or strange invaders. But it also carries the seeds of destruction within itself, since its extinction is foreshadowed by absolute war, a theme of many 'futuristic' romances that will be considered later. But not only war, even the desire for utopian happiness may be seen to lead to mankind's immediate destruction, once materialistic happiness is supposed to be the only kind of happiness worth striving for. The sane evolutionary utopian sees mankind involved in a long upward struggle. Whenever utopian fanatics try to find a short cut, the result is an inversion of optimistic utopian thought. This is true of *1984*, where the result is the greatest possible suffering and collective insanity. In J. E. Flecker's *The Last Generation* the result is the death of mankind. Maddened by the continuous misery, the industrial workers revolt. By bitter experience they have been taught not to believe in progress. They think that existence is a joke played on them by an inscrutable destiny which they decide to cheat of its prey. The workers' king introduces absolute contraception all over the world. Mankind will not suffer any longer and the last generation will be able to enjoy utopian happiness in an earthly paradise:

> 'Joy then be with you, my people, for the granaries are full of corn and wine that I have laid up, sufficient for many years to come; joy be with you, since you are the last and noblest generation of

> mankind, and since Doctor Smith by his invention and I by my provision have enabled you to live not only without payment and without work (loud cheers from the galleries), but also with luxury and splendour, and with all the delights, and none of the dangers, of universal love.'[96]

This is certainly the most radical and easiest way to utopia yet imagined by any writer.

Universal euthanasia, slavery, and cruel extinction on the one hand, immortality, unimaginable bliss, and godlike attributes on the other, both are equally valid aspects of evolutionary utopian writing. Hopes and fears, wildest optimism and deepest pessimism stand opposed to each other. The utopian is never well balanced. In the optimistic mood, man is the absolute master:

> 'Life has ruthlessly broken down all obstacles and liquidated all failures and to-day in its highest form—civilized man—and me as his representative, she presses forward,' etc.[97]

In the pessimistic mood man is subjected to the most degrading slavery:

> ' "That's what we are now—just ants. Only——"
> "Yes?" I said.
> "We're eatable ants." '[98]

Sometimes the utopian is swept away by his ecstatic vision, reduced to incoherent stammering:

> 'Some day here and everywhere, Life of which you and I are but the anticipatory atoms and eddies, life will awaken indeed, one and whole and marvellous, like a child awakening to conscious life. . . . We shall be there then, all that matters of us, you and I . . .
> And it will be no more than a beginning, no more than a beginning.'[99]

On the other hand the imaginative writer envisages the end of mankind in sad dejection:

> 'I saw the vast Halls and Palaces of men falling in slowly, decaying, crumbling, destroyed by nothing but the rains and the touch of Time. And looking again I saw wandering over and above the ruins, moving curiously about, myriads of brown, hairy, repulsive little apes.'[100]

These extremes are the final outcome of the original utopian conceptions: scientific humanism and the evolutionary creed. More's *Utopia* was mainly based on reason. His active humanistic temperament and the idea of Christian charity make it a duty to prevent suffering. It does not supply a new view of man in his relation to the universe. In Bacon's *New Atlantis* the position has slightly changed. Although the old view is by no means superseded, for the first time in utopian writing the idea of progress is expressed, the idea of the infinite perfectibility of man and of his power over other forms of life. Bacon's ideas were not strikingly developed till the second half of the nineteenth century, when they received official sanction and a new application by the evolutionary hypothesis. Since then there has been a continuous stream of evolutionary utopias, providing the adequate imaginative optimistic world-picture for all the merely melioristic social utopias. But while gaining a new independent significance and importance in the optimistic evolutionary view, man was at the same time reduced to a new insignificance by the awareness of the immense stretches of time in front of him and of the vast spaces around him. This new extension of the utopian view has necessarily led to ecstatic visions on the one hand and the deepest anxiety on the other. It is useless to disapprove of such forecasts by calling them fantastic. If the exercise of the long range utopian imagination is legitimate, it cannot be anything but fantastic, or rather, apocalyptic. Our minds have been so conditioned by the evolutionary view that it is impossible to imagine that mankind will not undergo the most extraordinary changes in the far future. If such changes are a development of all that is best in present man, there will be supermen, godlike creatures. If the changes take place without any qualitative direction, man in the far future will be so very different and strange that his world would seem a nightmare to us. And, furthermore, if mankind will be unable to move on from this earth, it also seems fairly certain that it will vanish and leave no trace of its existence in the world of time and space.

Is the use of such an evolutionary imagination legitimate? If literature is more than a merely playful and entertaining use of words, if it is to express deep human desires, hopes, fears, and insights, then evolutionary forecasts are as legitimate as Dante's *Divina Commedia.* That no work of great quality has been produced is no argument against the essential justification of an evolutionary utopia. It is certain that it is a highly significant and living modern myth. The subject being a vast religious myth, it should be treated poetically. Realistic prose fiction, with scientific arguments and explanations as in Wells's and Stapledon's works, does not seem to be the proper medium. They and others are well aware of the limitations imposed by such pedestrianism; but they hardly ever succeed in escaping from it. Wells occasionally does so in his more nightmarish forecasts. This failure may have to be explained by the fact that the evolutionary world-picture appeals only to the more scientific and abstract minds, while writers with a less theoretical approach need other subjects for inspiration. If the evolutionary creed does not sink deep into man's consciousness in times to come, there does not seem to be much hope that the 'evolutionary bible', as Shaw calls it, or even an evolutionary Pilgrim's Progress will be written. But the possibility should not be ruled out.

While the evolutionary fantasy is the only effective way of imaginatively dealing with the far future, the conservative, anti-utopian view makes a more plausible appeal when the near future is considered. It is only on this ground that anti-evolutionary forecasts can compete with their opposed prototypes. In such a case, anti-evolutionary and anti-progressive satires like G. K. Chesterton's fantasies or Ronald Knox's *Memories of the Future* prove effective weapons; and the view underlying such works seems a valid criticism of the optimistic evolutionary view:

> 'I wish I knew what it all meant. But I think this: I think it is the result of man being born immortal, and thinking (like an ass) that he has only this world to satisfy his immortal instinct with. Despairing of immortality in this world, and forgetting it in the next, he makes the human race the immortal unit, and so endows it with life. And, because he has been told that life means growth, he cannot be happy until he believes that the world in which he lives is growing, from something to something else. That is human vanity's favourite dogma, and there is no atom of proof for it. Everything we know about history and natural history shows that there is a kind of progress in the world from the less to the more complicated, from the less to the more organized: nothing suggests, except our vanity, that there is a progress from the worse to the better—and what other kind of progress would any sensible person give a tinker's curse for? That's it, I believe. Sweating away on the treadmill, humanity fancies that it is mountaineering, and that the dawn is just going to show above the next slope.'[101]

This criticism is especially applicable to a shorter time range, the hope to see the dawn above the next slope. Therefore it affects the social planning utopias much more than the evolutionary myth.

Generally people are inclined to agree that man is a higher and more valuable form of life than the amoeba, but they are not so certain whether present man is essentially superior to an ancient Greek. And the social utopias raise entirely new problems which will have to be dealt with in the next chapter.

Part Two

SOCIAL CONFLICTS

I

UTOPIA, ARCADIAN AND SCIENTIFIC

THE utopian imagination cannot remain content with far-off bliss and perfection. It is characterized by an insatiable desire to pull heaven down to earth by a violent effort. It not only wants to effect a radical change here, it also wants it now, if possible. Therefore a utopia generally presents a picture of an imaginary society whose standard, in the author's opinion, ought to or might be reached by the young readers' generation within their own lifetime, or at least within a period not exceeding the time span of recorded history.

The philosophical background, the evolutionary setting give the utopian hypothesis real significance by raising it above the level of playful speculation. Without the support of such an idea utopias had a weakened impact, or struck the reader as merely absurd and amusing, however clever. With its support they have been able to raise hope or strike terror in his heart. The stronger this evolutionary basis, the more convincing, plausible, and solid the respective picture of an imaginary society will appear; but a utopia will nevertheless be meaningless, if its social myth does not appeal to the reader's imagination and carry conviction in itself. The reader's imagination is worked on by the satisfaction of his deep longing for happiness. But, as we have seen, the mere satisfaction of such a desire only suffices to create the dream of an earthly paradise. Relying on the force of biological evolution in this case is of no use, since the creator of social utopias is concerned with the moral and social evolution of man. The time range is shorter, there is not so much room for the miraculous. The reader wants to be convinced that the utopian society is going to work under conditions which can be developed by present man's effort and intelligence. Therefore the range of the utopian imagination is severely restricted. The writer of social utopias of the near future has to compromise with reality in a way unknown to the creator of evolutionary myths. The original image of godlike man recedes. His creative effort can only achieve the greatest general happiness in a state which convinces the reader as being practicable. His ideal myth of utopian felicity has to be supported by a substructure of realistic logical argument. In time the demands of the realistic substructure become more and more imperative. The rift between the ideal and the real begins to show more and more clearly. Finally there is disintegration and perversion.

In pursuing their search for the best possible society the utopians have generally adopted two conflicting attitudes, two traditionally opposed views of man's position in this world: some of them hold that man is created and conditioned by his surroundings, others hold that man's mind is free. In the materialistic view, improving the environment will predominate since, with improved surroundings, man's mental progress will follow as a matter of course. If everybody is materially satisfied, everybody will be happy and behave like a Christian. The idealists on the other hand always insist on a primacy of man's mental and moral improvement. If all people are good, all will love each other, and material satisfaction will be the almost automatic consequence. These two extremes are often mixed in utopian practice. Moral, intellectual, and material improvement are seen working together and contributing to each other. All the same two clearly distinct types of utopia emerge, for the two fundamentally different aims require different initial conditions, which in their turn lead to diametrically opposite societies. These two types can be called arcadian and scientific.

In a sense every utopia is scientific. For in utopian writing we have not only to consider the contrast between realism and fantasy, but also the conflict between political pragmatism and utopian experimentalism. The first pursues a policy of muddling through, live and learn; the other trusts to methodical invention and conscious planning. The utopians first analyse the given conditions in society, and from the findings they construct, with all the knowledge available, a new society as near their ideal as possible. So in More's work analysis precedes reconstruction, though not in time of composition. Thus far all constructive utopias are more or less scientific in method. Engels's distinction between Socialism, Scientific and Utopian, is misleading. His 'scientific' socialism might just as well be called utopian. The difficulty with utopias is that they have hardly ever been properly tested. If there are no internal inconsistencies, only a practical test could decide whether any one kind of social planning is scientific or 'utopian'.

All the same, though most utopias show signs of scientific detachment, it is well to distinguish between scientific and arcadian utopias. For in the arcadian utopia the scientific method, the thought applied to the building of utopia, is used to abolish every kind of scientifically rigid construction within utopia. Anarchy and a sublimated state of nature are proclaimed. These utopias have been 'organized' in such a way that organization is no longer necessary. This is unrealistic even though corresponding to the Marxian view.

> 'The first act by virtue of which the State really constitutes itself the representative of the whole of society—the taking possession of the means of production in the name of society—this is, at the same time, its last independent act as State. State interference in social relations becomes, in one domain after another, superfluous, and then dies out by itself; the government of persons is replaced by the administration of things, and by the conduct of processes of production. The State is not "abolished". *It dies out.*'[102]

The same tendency is clearly noticeable in Morris's *News from Nowhere.* Not only are social relations almost entirely free of regulation; even production is no longer organized. Blatchford's *Sorcery Shop* is even more unrealistic, although it pretends to be strictly practical. The population keeps spontaneously turning out in the right numbers, on the right spot, at the right time, to do the right job, which is simply fantastic. Such a thing might possibly be imagined in arcadian surroundings in a patriarchal age, as pictured in Hudson's *Crystal Age.* But then the utopia becomes unrealistic because its arcadianism cannot be applied to modern society. Therefore these modern arcadian anarchies are not very numerous.[103]

The scientific utopia on the other hand accepts the fact that man is no longer in a state of nature, that a modern society has to be complex, and that its organization requires a great deal of social planning. In working this out the scientific utopian is led to use a considerable amount of applied science in order to deal adequately with a modern complex society which possibly extends over the whole world. The serious social planner generally tries to pursue some middle course, but by this very reasonableness he ceases to be utopian. The utopian imagination is clearly dominated by the idea of a scientific Brave New World on the one hand and the rural beautiful arcadian dream of a Crystal Age on the other.

Both myths are significant, but the scientific clockwork utopia possesses a higher degree of reality, embodying modern man's real hopes and fears. The arcadian Utopia nowadays has hardly ever any other function than reactionary wish-fulfilment, even when proposing ideals that seem far more desirable than the ones advocated in the scientific constructions.

> 'A highly organized and regimented society, whose members exhibit a minimum of personal peculiarities and whose collective behaviour is governed by a single masterplan imposed from above, is felt by the planners and even (such is the power of propaganda) by the plannees to be more "scientific", and therefore better, than a society of independent, truly cooperating and self-governing individuals.'[104]

It is felt to be more scientific because it can be demonstrated in detail how it is going to work, while in the other case matters have to be left to chance to a much greater extent. It is more 'scientific' because it treats man like material, and finally it is also felt to be more 'scientific' because it forms a continuation of what is happening and has been happening for some time. A continuation seems more plausible than a reaction because this course appears to offer the least resistance.

> 'It will be seen that at each point Burnham is predicting a continuation of the thing that is happening. Now the tendency to do this is not only bad habit like inaccuracy or exaggeration, which can be corrected by taking thought. It is a major mental disease, and its roots lie partly in cowardice and partly in the worship of power, which is not fully separable from cowardice.'[105]

But Orwell's *1984* is precisely a continuation of what is happening, and it has succeeded in impressing readers more than any other recent forecast just because it is so deeply rooted in what is happening. However, a simple continuation is not enough. What matters is the choice of a significant theme. There can be no doubt that the most significant theme for the modern utopian imagination and its mythology consists in the concept of scientific organization and the reaction against it.

> 'We all have this ambivalent attitude to planning to a greater or less degree, however good a face we may put on it, for we are all children of an age of transition, in which two kinds of motives are combined: the liberal distaste for meddling in human affairs,

and the passion for experiment marking a social age, which wants to explore the new possibilities of human nature.'[106]

Now it would be well to distinguish in brief the social conflicts inherent in contemporary scientific civilization in utopian perspective.

2

SCIENCE AND RELIGION

THE rise of utopianism and the rise of science run almost parallel. They are the outcome of a similar view of life. The emergence of utopia coincides with periods of scientific discovery and with ages that are experimental and critical in spirit. Greek utopianism represents the first stage, the Renaissance the second more enduring and fruitful one. More's *Utopia* stands on the threshold of scientific utopianism. Like Plato's *Republic* it is almost purely socially and morally constructive. Science itself plays a very small part indeed in it. More has no utopian scientific imagination. It is true, the Utopians incubate eggs artificially, but this is a mere picturesque detail. The Utopians also invent all kinds of machines for purposes of war: 'Engines for warre they devyse and invent wonders wittelye.'[107] But they do not profit from them in any noticeable degree, and the courses of study pursued by the Utopians are medieval, consisting of the trivium and quadrivium.

Christianopolis and *New Atlantis* mark a turning point. They introduce experimental science into utopia. The importance of inventions has been clearly realized by Bacon. Printing, gunpowder, and the compass 'have changed the appearance and the state of the whole world; first in literature, then in warfare, and lastly in navigation; and innumerable changes have thence derived, so that no empire, sect, or star appears to have exercised a greater power or influence on human affairs than these mechanical discoveries'.[108]

But in spite of all the amazing machines that are described by the member of the House of Solomon, *New Atlantis* remains a primitive scientific utopia. The joy in knowing, imitating, and outdoing nature is generally self-sufficient. There are engines serving for insulation, refrigeration, conservation, imitation; there are houses for 'deceits of the senses'. Animals are made bigger or smaller than their natural size, etc., etc. Social application of these inventions is vague. We are only told 'that of the things before recited many are grown into use throughout the kingdom.'[109] Only one practical purpose definitely emerges: the preservation of health. Although full of utopian science, *New Atlantis* is not an imaginative effort to see how science might affect and change society. The same lack of social purpose is noticeable in other scientific 17th century utopias, e.g. in the Countess of Newcastle's *Blazing World*. There is even a retrograde movement in the 18th century: distrust of civilization produces a spate of arcadian utopias where science has no place.

In the 19th century technical progress has become dominant, but with all its ugly appurtenances of Coketown it is hardly an object for utopian enthusiasm. The better-known English 19th century utopias are reactions against this squalid stage of the industrial development. *Erewhon*, *News from Nowhere*, *A Crystal Age*, all turn away from the machine. But significantly the machine itself is not completely destroyed in *News from Nowhere*, the most practical of these forecasts. There is an outward return to a state of nature, but the machine still fulfils a social function:

> 'All work which would be irksome to do by hand is done by immensely improved machinery, and in all work which is a pleasure to do by hand machinery is done without.'[110]

This is an anticipation of a later industrial stage, where noiseless efficiency and cleanness prevail; the hydro-electric power station opposed to the noisy smoking steam engine. Science is a servant, performing its duties like some kind of magic attendant, but there is no attempt to explain how the magic works:

> 'I understood pretty well that these "force vehicles" had taken the place of our old steam-power carrying; but I took good care not to ask any questions about them, as I knew well enough both that I should never be able to understand how they were worked, and that in attempting to do so I should betray myself, or get into some complication impossible to explain; so I merely said, "Yes of course, I understand".'[111]

Other minor English 19th-century utopias are similarly evasive. It is the American Bellamy who produces the first completely technological utopia. There immensely improved machinery is important at every stage. It is no longer just accepted, but considered as a positive value, even as a source of pleasure. *Looking Backwards* expresses a naïve belief in the spiritual efficiency of technical wonders. When faced with a radio-like gadget the visitor is completely overwhelmed:

> ' "It appears to me, Miss Leete," I said, "that if we could have devised an arrangement for providing everybody with music in their homes, perfect in quality, unlimited in quantity, suited to every mood, and beginning and ceasing at will, we should have considered the limit of human felicity already attained, and ceased to strive for further improvements".'[112]

With this utopia, machinery has come to stay as an integral part of all modern utopias, whether critical or constructive. Even in such an anti-metropolitan utopia as *The Wild Goose Chase*, which is designed to destroy mechanical devilishness, the hero condemns the wholesale destruction of machinery:

> 'But without the machines in this town we shall be able to do none of all this, and it is sentimentality or madness to talk of destroying them.'[113]

Technical advancement provides one of the main sources for fantastic entertainment. Aeroplanes, rockets, houses, food, everything becomes a fitting subject for utopian scientific fantasy, even with religious apologists like R. H. Benson.

Wells is the great protagonist of this modern tendency. He takes the development a stage further than the others and attempts a new synthesis. *New Atlantis* was a utopia of scientific research; *Looking Backwards* a utopia of socialized technology. Wells creates a *Modern Utopia* which is evolutionary not only in its social aspects, but also in its technics. Scientific research and socially applied science are combined; the machine moves on and on towards ever greater perfection. This progress is continued by modern utopian writers like Charlotte Haldane in *Man's World* (1926) and Viscount Samuel in *An Unknown Land* (1942). Beneficent effects result, the slavery of labour is more and more reduced, the standard of living reaches unprecedented heights.

> 'The plain message physical science has for the world at large is this, that were our political and social and moral devices only as well contrived to their ends as a linotype machine, an antiseptic operation plant, or an electric tram-car, there need now at the present moment be no appreciable toil in the world, and only the smallest fraction of the pain, the fear, and the anxiety that now makes human life so doubtful in its value. There is more than enough for everyone alive. Science stands, a too competent servant, behind her wrangling underbred masters, holding out

resources, devices, and remedies they are too stupid to use. And on its material side a modern Utopia must needs present these gifts as taken, and show a world that is really abolishing the need of labour, abolishing the last base reason for anyone's servitude or inferiority.'[114]

Such is the optimistic belief in technical progress. On the other hand hardly anyone is nowadays unaware of the dangers inherent in such a technological development. Soon technical progress becomes one of the favourite themes on which the utopian pessimist exercises his imagination. The harmful effects may be manifold, and so are the reactions against them. Corresponding to the machine wreckers of early industrialism we have utopian machine wreckers. Some of them, generally the more superficial ones, oppose the machines and industry on aesthetic grounds. In a utopia like *A Crystal Age* the machines have been abolished because of their ugliness and the crudity of their products.

For others the machine is evil in itself, even if it were clean and beautiful. No matter what the economical and social results it is bad because it has a certain existence of its own. In such a view the machine is no longer just a tool. It runs and 'wants' to be kept running. It becomes necessary, it needs attendants, there will be more and more machines, there will be machines to produce other machines. The more machines there are the more will be needed, till man's freedom is threatened. In the Erewhonian *Book of the Machines* this threat is exploited in evolutionary terms, in order to make it more effective. As we have seen in the first chapter, the idea of being superseded in the biological struggle is intolerable to man. If it can be proved that machines have consciousness, man is able to realize the threat in his imagination and the machines will have to be destroyed completely. This 'proof' is furnished by Butler's subtle argumentation.

Generally the utopians' approach is not so argumentative as that of Samuel Butler. They prefer the concreter and more striking way of presenting machines already endowed with life. Simultaneously with Butler, Bulwer-Lytton made use of this device:

'A figure in a simpler garb than that of my guide, but of similar fashion, was standing motionless near the threshold. My guide touched it twice with his staff, and it put itself into a rapid and gliding movement, skimming noiselessly over the floor. Gazing on it, I then saw that it was no living form, but a mechanical automaton.'[115]

There is no need whatever to give a human shape to a highly complicated machine. Other forms would probably be far more functional. But it is this shape which gives symbolic expression to the high degree of perfection reached by the machines and to the evolutionary threat. Therefore robots are one of the stock themes of utopian fantasy and have become specially frequent since Karel Capek's play *R.U.R.* (Rossum Universal Robots), where the term robot was used for the first time (1923). In Alun Llewellin's *The Strange Invaders* (1934) and in Lord Dunsany's *The Last Revolution* (1951) the threat of the machine is expressed in its most striking form: the revolt of the robots, the machine coming alive and actually dominating man.

Other less fantastic ways are open to the utopian writer. There may be an exaggerated accumulation of machinery that in itself seems either absurd or frightening.[116] More impressive than such superficial amusing skits are utopias where machinery impresses by its ruthless efficiency, where man really seems to exist in order to serve and feed machinery.

> 'Under the balcony this extraordinary roadway ran swiftly to Graham's right, an endless flow rushing along as fast as a nineteenth-century express train, an endless platform of narrow transverse overlapping slats with little interspaces that permitted it to follow the curvatures of the street. Upon it were seats, and here and there little kiosks, but they swept by too swiftly for him to see what might be therein. From this nearest and swiftest platform a series of others descended to the centre of the space. Each moved to the right, each perceptibly slower than the one above it, but the difference in pace was small enough to permit anyone to step from any platform to the one adjacent, and so walk uninterruptedly from the swiftest to the motionless middle way. And seated in crowds upon the two widest and swiftest platforms, or stepping from one to another down the steps, or swarming over the central space, was an innumerable, a wonderfully diversified multitude of people.'[117]

The passage describes efficient transportation and organization, but that is not the dominant impression left in the reader's mind. Hurling masses, rushing pavements point to the threatening windvanes, pursuing helicopters, twisting cables, blaring loudspeakers, flashing lights that make their appearance later in the book. The hero is completely swallowed up in this highly efficient mechanical organization, which is so overwhelming that it seems to turn into an inimical organism, a mad monster. Although it does not rely on fantastic symbolism, the whole book is a prolonged technical nightmare.

The persistent fear of the machine takes another, subtler form in the shape of technocracies. In Bacon's utopia the philosopher is no longer the king. His place has been taken by the research scientist, whose power and glory are celebrated on the grand scale. Technocracy is at work in Bellamy's state, and even more so in Wells's forecasts, in *Brave New World*, in *The Wild Goose Chase*, and in Olaf Stapledon's Americanized technological world state in *Last and First Men*.

There the most modern technical symbol, the aeroplane, becomes the yardstick of human value and worldly rewards. Only a skilful pilot can hope for a satisfactory social position and 'legal sexual freedom'. Those who cannot pass the first test are not even allowed to marry. Finally a fanatical worship of movement for its own sake is derived from machinery. Progress and movement are identified. The more movement, the better. This tendency expresses itself in 'devotional aerial acrobatics', because in such exercises the maximum of movement is achieved.[118]

All these robot revolutions, worlds of machinery, and technocracies express the fear of man becoming enslaved and dominated by machinery in a direct and melodramatic way. Just as Graham, *The Sleeper*, is threatened by wind-wheels, cables, searchlights, and helicopters on his flight across the giant roof of the city, modern man is threatened by the machine in an almost physical sense.

But another danger arises when machinery and technics are so efficient and cleverly organized that man seems practically independent and freed from physical hazards. Then he can devote his time and energy to what seems essential. Then man in his material independence becomes more and more godlike.

> 'As he approaches more to the alleged god-like stage, man will live more and more alone, meeting his fellow creatures at comparatively rare intervals.'[119]

There is no need to meet because of amazing technical means of communication.

> 'Even marriage may become automatic. In an age of universal wireless and television, it will seem absurd for a dozen different clergymen or registrars in different parts of the country to have to say the same words and ask identical questions.'

> 'If cranks and levers do away with local colour it is that "Colour" which is at fault.'[120]

In E. M. Forster's *The Machine Stops* improved communication leads to such a new splendid isolation. Mother and son are living in the inside of the earth, communicating thousands of miles apart. The mother has hundreds of acquaintances, whom she 'meets' by means of television-phone. But her son wants to visit her at the cost of his life. He is not satisfied with a technical second best, with a substitute for reality.

Here technology seems to be the perfect unobtrusive servant of man. Nevertheless it is attacked because it is an obstacle between man and reality. Science and the machine produce the substitute. Artificially condensed food has been invented as early as *New Atlantis*. Bacon's joy in imitating nature for imitation's sake in houses for 'deceits of the senses', opens the way for thrills instead of genuine experiences. Later Bellamy comes forward with his specious arguments for substitute music. Finally in *Brave New World* everything has become substitute. It is the society of perfectly applied science. *Our Ford* is symbolical. Science and society have been amalgamated. In birth, in character formation, in emotional experience, in aesthetic perception, everywhere, we have the substitute instead of the real thing. It is not a matter of man being enslaved, but of man being killed. The opening is characteristic:

> 'The enormous room on the ground floor faced towards the north. Cold for all the summer beyond the panes, for all the tropical heat of the room itself, a harsh thin light glared through the windows, hungrily seeking some draped lay figure, some pallid shape of academic goose-flesh, but finding only the glass and nickel and bleakly shining porcelain of a laboratory. Wintriness responded to wintriness. The overalls of the workers were white, their hands gloved with a pale corpse-coloured rubber. The light was frozen, dead, a ghost. Only from the yellow barrels of the microscopes did it borrow a certain rich and living substance, lying along the polished tubes like butter, streak after luscious streak in long recession down the work tables.
> "And this", said the Director opening the door, "is the Fertilizing Room".'[121]

There is death instead of life. The origin of life itself is dead. The end is reached when an independent revolutionary soul like Winston Smith in *1984* is crushed by a combination of argument and applied science. What is Orwell's Room 101 but Bacon's house for 'the deceit of the senses' applied practically? Bacon's *Merchants of Light* have made possible Orwell's 'room where there is no darkness', where man is transformed beyond recognition. Things do not remain a mystery any longer. Nature is turned into an object for experiments. The natural scale of values disappears. Ethical relativism takes its place. Science becomes absolute. In Charlotte Haldane's *Man's World* the research scientist, the hero, takes special pleasure in having his brain exposed and analysed.

Man is not considered as a being with a soul but as a bundle of nerves and reflexes. Pain and suffering lose their meaning. The scientist turns madly inhuman. Wells's attitude again is ambivalent, even here where research is regarded. In *The Island of Dr. Moreau*, the scientist experimenting on animals, making them half human, is insane. In Rex Warner's *Wild Goose Chase* the research institute becomes the scene of ultimate nightmarish horror.

The sinister powerful insane scientist has become a favourite theme of popular imagination, and the utopian fantasies are full of them. They may not be insane from the 'scientific' point of view, of course, but from the merely human one. 'They' are at work in *1984* as well as in C. S. Lewis's fantasies. Just like the devil, the sorcerer, and the witch in former ages, nowadays the scientist, preferably the insane scientist, lurks behind everything. Fear of the scientific villain seems to be a kind of modern persecution mania. Todd's *Lost Traveller* somehow suddenly finds himself in an entirely different country. There is a glaring sun, a desert full of diamonds. The sun does not move. First he thinks he has gone mad, but a modern Lost Traveller can still have recourse to another explanation: 'They' are at work.

> 'They must have been cunning to dump him in the midst of timelessness and to escape themselves. Presumably they were the master-criminals of the thrillers, who had the services of brilliant scientists, kinked, at their command.'[122]

Arcadian utopias reject all science of this description. But the most significant and important attack is not content with a fuller humanistic realization of aesthetic and creative experiences. Man must be considered as a spiritual being first. Opposed to the utopian scientific view there is the anti-utopian religious view. We have seen that transcendental religion was not favourable to the rise of utopia. What then is the role of religion in a modern utopia? Are there religious utopias?

In More's Utopia religion is important but by no means dominant. It is not a co-ordinating factor. But Campanella's *City of the Sun* and Andreae's *Christianopolis* as well as Samuel Gott's *Nova Solyma* are based on religion.[123] They are theocracies, the church taking the place of the secular authority of the state. Doubtless the church is orientated towards a different end, not towards secular happiness, but towards the saving of souls; but its authority in utopia can be just as oppressive, often dictatorial. Characteristically there is no real Protestant theocratic utopia because Protestantism is too individual. The Catholic utopia of Campanella and the Protestant one of Andreae are very different. Andreae's is much more liberal, and not much concerned with practical organization. In Samuel Gott's *Nova Solyma* there is even less of it.

Modern English religious utopias have mostly been written by converts to Catholicism. The basis for such utopias is provided by a church with stricter organization and by the added zeal of converts. An approach to a Catholic world domination is depicted in Fr. Rolfe's (Baron Corvo's) *Hadrian VII* (1904). This is mainly the outcome of a personal power dream; the imaginary pope (Fr. Rolfe) reorganizes the political world by means of his magnetic personal influence. A Catholic utopia on more traditional lines is described in R. H. Benson's *Dawn of All* (1911). The world is dominated by Catholicism. The last few recalcitrant Socialists are shipped to Bellamy's Massachusetts. Ireland has become a centre of spiritual life. Science and religion are reconciled. In Lourdes miracles have been completely industrialized. Everywhere the old kingdoms have been re-established.[124]

In spite of such attempts, a religious utopia remains a *contradictio in adjecto*, for the religious organization is only a means to a transcendental end. A truly religious utopia is Heaven, or an Earthly Paradise, and should not depict this world, but the next. But such paramount bliss can hardly be described and a description would be considered sacrilegious. Only the *Divine Comedy* might possibly be called a truly religious utopia. Sometimes the journey to paradise is presented in allegorical form, but the description ends when the golden city is reached, as in *Pilgrim's Progress*. C. S. Lewis's *The Great Divorce* is a modern instance of such a journey of the soul towards perfection in another world, while *Out of the Silent Planet* is a more genuine spiritual utopia. There people live in constant religious consciousness and commune with the deity in a way that surpasses anything possible on earth, the 'silent planet'.

Herbert Read's *The Green Child* is the most original and impressive of the spiritual utopias. The green underworld is organized in a social way, but there is no possibility of applying its system to the problems of our real world. It is neither a religious world in the orthodox sense, nor is it just fantastic. In the green country there is constant individual progression towards ever higher perfection from active joyful youth to contemplative age. But in spite of strictly ordered hierarchical progression towards spiritual discipline, the sense of time is absent. This underground timeless utopia is the intermediate stage between Maia and Nirvana. The sages end their lives in caves contemplating eternal harmony while ringing all the possible changes on a limited number of finely cut crystals.

But such a work is rather the exception than the rule. Generally the religious idea and the spiritual life of the individual are not shown as dominant in a utopia. Their appeal appears stronger when we see the spiritual and religious forms in dramatic opposition to the scientific progressive socialized machine age. The writer is on the side of the Lost Cause against modern science. He purposely makes his cause the Lost Cause because it becomes more impressive and moving than when it is winning. It secures the reader's sympathy while the practical difficulties of social organization need not be faced. R. H. Benson has written two utopian novels dealing with conflicts between the Catholic church and anti-religious socialism. *Lord of the World* (1907) ends with the defeat and complete annihilation of the Catholic church at the hands of the representatives of the Religion of Mankind, a kind of evolutionary Socialism. This story of a defeat is far more successful than the idealized picture and propaganda of *The Dawn of All* (1911). A writer cannot be so biased and obviously satirical when his own cause loses. The opposing force may be hateful, it is true, but the author cannot make it weak and ridiculous in addition. Because he sees it successful he has to search deeper, he has to give genuine reasons for its success. He has to make a convincing case, which will appear all the more plausible because it is clear that he is not on its side. Consequently there is greater artistic balance, a real conflict. All this is easily lost if the author strongly sympathizes with the victorious cause. The enemy is doubly disposed of. He is proved to be weak and wrong at the same time. First the author makes him appear weak and defeated because he thinks him wrong. Then he implies that the enemy is wrong because he appears weak, since the right and more intelligent cause will always triumph. A few opposing arguments are often added to give a semblance of fairmindedness.

The technique of the satiric foil is adopted in most utopias. The anti-utopian crank is used as a convenient means of discrediting existing institutions. In More's *Utopia* for instance, there are the foolish vain visitors. In Wells's *Modern Utopia* we encounter the grumbling apostle of nature who is not at all satisfied with the utopian state of affairs, etc., etc. Very often such satire is far too obvious and crude. In a very minor utopia like Ollivant's *To-morrow* the anti-utopian, 'Jax, the Atavist' becomes an absurdly subhuman creature.

This crude partiality is avoided when the author is siding with the Lost Cause, as in *Brave New World* or *Concrete*.[125] At the most the author's convictions are expressed in the form of a small reactionary settlement where no social problems have to be dealt with. In *Concrete* science rules the world, but a small Christian community called Cambridge still exists on a small Pacific island. In *Ape and Essence* there is a similar ideal colony, but the author takes care that the reader gets no close view of it. So the reader easily forgets that the Lost Cause might not really be desirable if it were dominant. Because the Lost Cause is defended with a certain tragic dignity this should make us think that it is good in itself.

But the opposing attitude may also be treated quite neutrally. In *Man's World*, one of the least satirical modern utopias, a genuine dramatic conflict arises between the new science and the imaginative religious man.[126] The problem is fairly stated. There is simply no room for such a man in a utopian scientific society. This is tragic as far as the individual is concerned, since this religious, imaginative approach embodies real values, but it is shown to be necessary as far as the evolution of the human race is concerned. The stating of the problem is more important than the didactic or satirical purpose. In this respect *Man's World* is very exceptional indeed.

Brave New World and *Man's World* most clearly summarize the conflict between the scientific rationalist view on the one hand and the religious and artistic view on the other. The problem is considered from different angles but the conclusion is the same: scientific humanism in its most extreme form is completely victorious. Religious and artistic life is exiled or pushed underground to some imaginary inner world as in Herbert Read's *Green Child.*

3

MASS AND CLASS

In the utopian nightmare science and technology are freed from ordinary restrictions. They enslave and crush man. The ordinary human being as well as the scientist appear tied to the machine, working away and not getting anywhere, like the research-worker in Aldous Huxley's *Antic Hay*. The social consequences may be even more frustrating and inescapable. Science affects technics and technics in their turn affect the social structure. The resulting development assumes the proportions of an avalanche engulfing mankind. Science and technology further the rise of the machine; machinery makes industries possible; industrialism creates mass populations. Mass populations necessitate scientific management and organization. These in their turn will employ more science, more machinery, etc., etc.

But once scientific organization sets in, this development need not go on for ever. The population may be artificially stabilized. All the same, modern utopias are forced to deal with mankind in the mass. This may make utopian planning more complicated, but at the same time it favours utopian generalizations. In the mass, man as a responsible particular citizen vanishes. The bigger the figures are, the smaller the value attached to the individual will be. Sympathetic imagination is baffled by the very size of the numbers. The mass material cannot form itself into an organic shape, but cries out for utopian moulding.

Two different utopian views of scientific humanism emerge: on the one hand there is Mankind, a symbol of the highest value. It is the religious unit within which the individual achieves eternal significance. As a member of it he is in touch with the Superman. He equals God. On the other hand there is Man in the Mass. The mass is also mankind, but mankind at a definite historical moment, in a special social situation. It is not yet in the inspired state, it does not attain the higher consciousness of Wellsian citizens of the future, or the racial ecstasy of Stapledon's Last Men. Such ideal men lose their identity to find themselves reunited in some common higher being.

But man in the mass loses his identity without compensation. If he does find himself united with some force, this can only be described as some common lower being. As an evolutionary unit, utopian man identifies himself with the Superman, as a social unit he is in danger of becoming a Subman.

In the utopian imagination the subman does not appear as an individual, but as part of a more comprehensive unit. The interdependence of science, technics, industrialization, mass population, and social organization is figuratively expressed by the striking symbol of the Giant Town. In one way or another most modern utopias are haunted by it. Formerly it was not important. In Plato's and More's time the city state and the small town perfectly expressed the limits of utopian civilization. Towards the end of the nineteenth century the giant town makes its appearance; e.g. in Bellamy's Boston of *Looking Backwards*. For a nïave technical optimist like Professor Low the spreading of towns over as many square miles as possible spells the ultimate victory of progress:

> 'Evolution from the tiny collection of mud huts to the mighty centre of the future, covering many thousands of square miles, will continue gradually.'[127]

In Stapledon's *Last and First Men* very soon the whole world is urbanized. All the continents are studded with immense pylons, utopian Le Corbusier housing machines. In Wells's *Modern Utopia* London is the immense capital of a world state. Among many other institutions of adequate size there is a University with thousands of professors, tens of thousands of advanced students. In the middle of this giant city there is a huge central square:

> 'Great multitudes of people will pass softly to and fro in this central space, beautiful girls and youths going to the University classes that are held in the stately palaces about us, grave and capable men going to their businesses, children meandering to their schools.'[128]

The giant city of the future with all the calm leisureliness of arcadian *News from Nowhere*! The utopian need not be concerned with exact planning, it is true, but when such departures from plausibility occur we should like to know how such amazing results are achieved. We are not told.

Such beautiful dream cities with all the size and business of a giant town, but with none of its concomitant bustle, are exceptions in utopian literature. The typical utopian supertown is developed on more traditional lines. It resembles a preternaturally enlarged mechanized beehive.

> 'His first impression was one of overwhelming architecture. The place into which he looked was an aisle of Titanic buildings, curving spaciously in either direction. Overhead mighty cantilevers sprang together across the huge width of the place, and a tracery of translucent material shut out the sky. Gigantic globes of cold white shamed the pale sunbeams that filtered down through the girders and wires. Here and there a gossamer suspension bridge dotted with foot passengers flung across the chasm and the air was webbed with slender cables. A cliff of edifice hung above him, he perceived, as he glanced upward, and the opposite facade was grey and dim and broken by great archings, circular perforations, balconies, buttresses, turret projections, myriads of vast windows, and an intricate scheme of architectural relief.'[129]

Everything is on the gigantic scale. The roofing of the town is continuous. There is no real daylight. A good deal of the life is carried on underground. Moreover the town is sharply separated by huge walls from the surrounding country in order to stress the contrast between the outmoded individualistic life in the country and the mass population of the town. This contrast is even more clearly expressed in Wells's *Story of Days to Come*. Dissatisfied with the life in the town, a young couple are considering an act which is quite unheard of and which they hardly dare imagine: With the courage of despair they escape from the town into the mysterious, frightening country. But when they are there they are forced to realize that they are completely out of touch with nature. They decide to return to the slavery and the protection of the town rather than face the risks of country life.

In Rex Warner's *Wild Goose Chase* the giant town is similarly separated from everything that is natural.

> 'Looking in all directions George could not see the limit of the concrete roof, slit here and there for ventilation, with other towers, more than he had seen from the desert, rising to great heights in front of him and at each side.'[130]

Once man has stepped inside this town, he is caught and at the mercy of inimical, inhuman forces. He is haunted by a sense of claustrophobia. After his escape from this town the hero feels as if he had awakened from a nightmare.

> 'Stiff stood the blank walls of concrete, forbidding, and from within George could still hear the confused hubbub of a strange life, but except for the single constable outside the walls he was alone and, as he looked back on that enclosure and that laughing face, sights which were horrible to him, he felt free, at least for the time being, standing in acres of corn in a bright light that was surely of day.'[131]

The town has become the symbol of evil. In *1984* it enhances the effect of political oppression. Sometimes, as in *The Wild Goose Chase*, the town is destroyed by the vital forces of the country; sometimes it collapses as a consequence of an imaginary global war. In such fantasies of a relapse into barbarism the ruins of the giant town remind the remnants of humanity of a mysterious past civilization. In the *War in the Air* the hero is not understood when telling the young man about past town civilization. In *Overture to Cambridge* it is a crime to approach the ruins of the big towns. They are thought to be the seats of evil spirits because there is a dim tradition that the destruction of humanity has originated in these giant cities of the scientific age.

In real social planning several solutions are proposed by which the giant town can be avoided;[132] but at present the utopian imagination is preoccupied with the inhuman giant town, the symbol for the undifferentiated, uprooted mass. In the scientific forecasts, life is mass-produced in every sphere. Man is standardized. One individual can hardly be distinguished from the other. The scientific patterns for utopian man may be widely different; but more important than that is the fact that he has to conform to such a common pattern in each of them. They all depart from existing conditions in mass-producing a special type of man. In some modern utopias the frightening sameness of a standardized society is exaggerated in order to point out the dangers of a development laying too much stress on equality and identity. Such reactions are a comparatively late result of technical standardization, a twentieth-century phenomenon. Before, there had been conviction in the happy dream of a classless society in which all men were perfectly equal. Equality and identity seemed desirable. Social distinctions appeared dangerous because they were leading to class distinctions, which were considered pernicious. Such class distinctions have been violently attacked in a great number of utopian satires. Probably the best-known and most striking example is provided by Wells's *Time Machine*. After thousands of years the capitalists and the workers emerge as different species. The Eloi, the former capitalists, are reduced to a state of beautiful decadence, childishly playing about in marvellous old mansions. The Morlocks, the workers, are living underground in a world of machinery. By living in darkness for ages they have become blind and only come up by night to devour the Eloi, who are kept like cattle by the Morlocks. Generally these satires do not go to quite such fantastic lengths in condemning class distinctions. *The Sleeper Awakes* describes an overgrown future capitalist society. The workers are underprivileged. The blue overall is the symbol for the slavery of these masses, who are just allowed to vegetate. In Rose Macaulay's *Orphan Island* (1924) the same theme is treated in a lighter vein. The Smiths, descending from the pure English settlers, represent the Victorian capitalist ruling class, all non-Smiths are the disinherited subjects.

Often such strong class distinctions are only the initial situation for a utopian cautionary tale. The existing contrasts prove to be too marked for the well-being of a society. The authors want to demonstrate what must become of the old capitalist society if no changes are made in time. In the world of the *Time Machine* it is too late for any changes; but in many other cases the old class distinctions mark the beginnings of social revolutions. Most of these revolutionary stories tend to be rather sensational, full of violent action. The horrors of a class war are drastically presented and sometimes the social message recedes into the background. At the beginning of the twentieth century there are lots of sensational books describing England under terroristic Socialist regimes.[133]

Where the social message is more important than the sensational element, the class war remains an episode on the way to utopia. In most classically constructive utopias the story sets in long after the change has taken place. The utopian society described has achieved stability. All the innumerable practical difficulties of changing from one system to another are much more easily overcome than in attempts to describe the emergence of utopia at a close range. All the same Wells has also created some accounts of rising utopias. One of his most detailed histories is given in *The Holy Terror* (1939); but at the end the limits set by a novel only leave room for the description of a utopian dawn. In *The Shape of Things to Come* the change as well as the utopian organization are dealt with. The resulting production is somewhat cumbersome. It only proves that the traditional utopian method is to be preferred. This consists in presenting the change in the form of a historical flash-back. Germs of this method can be detected in More's and Bacon's work. By the time of Butler, Bulwer-Lytton, Morris, Bellamy, and Wells it has become established. These historical accounts frequently deal with events very summarily indeed. Sometimes, as in Bellamy's case, writers are unduly optimistic.

> 'Such a stupendous change [from private property to state ownership] as you describe", said I, "did not, of course, take place without great bloodshed and terrible convulsions". "On the contrary", replied Dr. Leete, "there was absolutely no violence. The change had been long foreseen. Public opinion had become fully ripe for it, and the whole mass of people was behind it. There was no more possibility of opposing it by force than by argument".'[134]

In *News from Nowhere* the change is far more violent and protracted. The starting point is the opposition of capital and labour. This contrast increases steadily till the revolution produces a new society. This society seems to work admirably, in arcadian surroundings. It is classless.

In the modern scientific mass-utopia on the other hand the distinction between the capitalist and the working class may be abolished; the society is standardized, but it is by no means classless. The classless society is essentially an 18th-century arcadian dream, the twentieth-century utopia has clear class distinctions. Wells's work may serve to illustrate this. Where he is creating an avowedly unrealistic picture, as in *Men Like Gods*, the society runs on the lines of classless arcadianism. But in a *Modern Utopia* he endeavours to be practical; classes re-emerge at once.

> 'The social theorists of Utopia, my double explained, did not base their schemes upon the classification of men into labour and capital, the landed interest, the liquor trade, and the like. They esteemed these as accidental categories, indefinitely amendable to statesmanship, and they looked for some practical and real classification upon which to base organisation. But on the other hand, the assumption that men are unclassifiable, because practically homogeneous, which underlies modern democratic methods and all the fallacies of our equal justice, is even more alien to the Utopian mind.'[135]

There are four classes: the Poetic, the Kinetic, the Dull, and the Base. The first are the leaders of mankind, the second the executives, the third are the workers, and the last class consists of socially antagonistic elements.

Classes re-emerge, but it is to be observed that they are not the old ones, which to a planner seem to be merely accidental. The new classes are 'scientific'. In this instance they are founded on a psychological basis. As regards society, these classes must be described as functional. A modern utopia is a utopia of functional hierarchy, like Plato's *Republic*. Wells himself is still rather moderate, even liberal, in applying this principle. There is not much regimentation, the classes somehow organize themselves, society is a living organism rather than a machinelike organization. In spite of employing scientific terms it is essentially anarchist. So *A Modern Utopia* is the first modern utopia; but at the same time the last modern utopia, for on the one hand it does away with the idea of a classless society, but on the other hand it is the last to present the society of functional classes in an attractive light. Others have continued to describe functional hierarchies, but their attitude has changed to one of pessimism. These pessimistic forecasts of strictly regimented societies must be considered the most important type of modern utopian fiction. They are far more numerous than either arcadian anarchies or scientific 'eutopias'.[136] In all of them there is a clash between the insight that a modern utopia has to be scientific and must be erected on a fairly rigid system of functional classes on the one hand, and between the deeply engrained liberal desire for individual freedom, equality, and personal dignity on the other. In the scientific utopias after Wells's *Modern Utopia* one always has the impression that man is caught in the social machine without any chance of extricating himself. Their effect is all the more depressing because they do not seem very far removed from contemporary reality. *1984*, for instance, is largely based on Burnham's interpretation of recent history as expounded in *The Managerial Revolution*. All these modern utopias deal with man in the mass. The mass is divided into classes. The sharpest possible division between the classes is combined with identity within one class. The number of these functional classes is restricted as much as possible. It generally varies between three and five, for the working out of a utopian formula would be too much complicated by an undue diversity. Each individual becomes one of innumerable identical class-atoms, while each class is one of the few indispensible elements in the utopian experiment carried out in the giant town.

4

THE SERVILE STATE

IN modern utopias the need for organization has become stronger than ever before, for they are necessarily conceived on a grander scale and are consequently more complicated than the old-fashioned ideal city states of former times. Therefore a modern utopia cannot be a state in which man would feel naturally happy, as he might possibly be in an arcadian one. He is hemmed in on every side. The utopian economic organization may be perfect, but the individual may not be satisfied with his political status. If he is tempted to revolt, the whole utopian structure is in danger. The most admirably constructed utopia fails to convince if we are not led to believe that the danger of revolt is excluded. The reader may fairly easily be convinced that the problems of organization have been solved efficiently; but he is far more sceptical where human nature is concerned. How is an ordinary man turned into a utopian citizen?

As a first means there are the perfect laws, which have to be strictly obeyed. In More's and in many other utopias offenders are severely punished. But this is a negative aspect, and utopian writers are generally careful to point out that such offences are extremely rare occurrences. Every appearance of undue coercion is avoided. The laws are there, it is true, but the utopian organization is meant to be a commonwealth of freely co-operating citizens, convinced of the essential goodness of their state.

> 'This is their sentence and opinion of virtue and pleasure. And they believe that by mans reason alone none can be found trewer than this.'[137]
>
> 'These and suchlike opinions have they conceaved, partely by education, beinge brought up in that commonwealth, . . . and partely by good literature and learning.'[138]

The force of public opinion is more important than the laws, and public opinion is influenced by education. The education is directed towards creating a perfectly functioning citizen much more than towards the forming of an independent mind. Among the early utopias this is specially noticeable in Plato's *Republic*:

> 'Our rulers will have to administer a great quantity of falsehood and deceit for the benefit of the ruled.'[139]

In More's *Utopia* the citizen's attitude is still formed and shaped by a political education; the citizen arrives at the insight that Utopia is better than other states by clear and generally acceptable reasoning; he is not conditioned by emotional propaganda, although there are certain trends towards a shaping of personality of conditioned reflexes. The Utopians' 'instinctive' disgust of gold has been achieved by such conditioning. But in More's *Utopia* this is a rather incidental matter.

Traditional utopias generally content themselves with influencing the individual with laws, force of public opinion, and education.[140] In the traditional small utopias this is sufficient. Every individual can see how utopia works and be satisfied with his own role within the organization. In the modern mass utopia this is no longer possible. In order to arrive at a working order that can easily be grasped and imagined, society is strictly stratified. This stratification on the one hand facilitates the working of utopia, on the other hand it might easily lead to a break-up of utopia by a revolution. The most striking example of such an imperfectly balanced utopia is provided by Wells's *The Sleeper Awakes*. The oppressed working classes and the exploiting capitalists are opposed to each other. Civil war results because the workers are suppressed by mere force. This is the type of a mass utopia not employing scientific means to safeguard its existence and continuity. The utopian leaders have not realized the problem. Men in a modern utopia are unequal, but the lower classes must not be suppressed by brutal force. The very source of dissatisfaction must be stopped. Man must be properly conditioned.

First utopia was designed to satisfy the needs of the 'average' man, within the restrictions imposed by contemporary conditions. In a modern utopia these restrictions are so severe that the needs of the average man do not appear to be satisfied; on the contrary, the citizen is designed to satisfy the needs of the utopian state. The original utopias were the best states because the citizens felt happy in them or because they at least safeguarded the greatest possible happiness of the greatest possible number. In a modern scientific utopia the citizens are told to be happy because they are members of a community labelled: 'Best State Possible'. Originally such an attempt might have appeared absurd. But in the scientific utopia cleverly exploited mass psychology steps in. It secures an infallible means of conditioning the utopian citizens to the utopian ideals. These ideals need no longer correspond to any absolute idea of good or the requirements of the citizens.

> 'The basis for a calculus of the achieved degree of goodness in a society or a cultural group will be, I believe, this principle: Societies are good in the degree to which they make possible the attainment of the ends which their citizens are taught to pursue.'[141]

The means have triumphed over the ends. Given some kind of working order for the utopian state it does not matter much what kind it is as long as the citizen can be persuaded that he is happy. The citizens' happiness in many modern utopias is the result of scientific mass suggestion. Another short cut to utopian happiness has been invented.

So it is not surprising that propaganda plays an important part in the modern utopian imagination. There are a great number of satires exploiting this theme in many variations. Newspapers and advertising come in for violent attacks.[142] In some of Wells's stories of the future, man is exposed to an increasing pressure. In the giant towns loudspeakers shout at the masses from every corner of every building. In *What Not* (1918) Rose Macaulay depicts a utopian propaganda campaign of immense co-ordination. A whole nation is whipped up into hysteria, all about intellectual improvement. The climax is achieved in Robert Nichols's *Golgatha & Co.* (1923). A future pauperized post-war world is divided into the very poor and the very rich. It is a world without hope and without the comforts of religion. Here and there workers are threatening to revolt. The supercapitalists meet and decide to deviate the suppressed energy of the people into the channels of religion. A puppet Messiah is created and launched on the world with astounding propaganda. Religious films are produced, the papers are full of articles and religious serials, books on the same subjects are published in great numbers, talks and meetings are arranged everywhere, and aeroplanes trace fiery crosses in the skies. Finally the crucifixion itself is to be re-enacted in an apocalyptic finale. Propaganda has become so important that it can afford the main theme for the utopian writer; but generally such propagandistic fantasies, though hardly ever absent from modern utopias, are subordinated to the central social theme.

However effective, 'straight propaganda' is generally considered hardly sufficient for utopian uses, because it is necessarily rather indiscriminately applied. There is no absolute guarantee that it will exercise the desired effect on the individual. Scientific conditioning is more closely controlled. With propaganda, although under a higher psychological pressure than with the education of an old-fashioned utopia, the independent and critical individual still has the possibility of escape; he may keep his own mind intact at least. But as long as there is an independent mind, utopian stability is in danger. There is only safety if any individual consciousness worth speaking of has been eliminated. So in Aldous Huxley's *Brave New World* the future utopian citizen is pre-natally and post-natally conditioned and completely fitted to the function which he will have to fulfil in later life. He is so conditioned that he will feel happy in this future role, and would be unhappy if any other kind of occupation and life were assigned to him.

One obstacle presents serious difficulties to the ingenuity of the utopian organizer. Ideas of freedom, equality, social justice, human dignity may be fairly easily disposed of in the utopian forecasts. But for a modern age it is not so easy to dispose of the instincts, especially the sexual instinct. Here at least man seems to be in touch with some ultimate reality transcending social planning. But even this instinct can be neutralized by proper utopian handling. Individual love and the satisfaction of the sexual urge are kept separate. Individual love, tending as it does to create independent social cells within the greater social body, is considered especially dangerous. At the same time it is less absolute a force than the indiscriminate sexual instinct. Therefore it is the first to disappear. As early as Plato's *Republic* sexual communism is enforced, at least among the ruling class. In many later ideal states sexual freedom is a matter of course, representing a desirable end, the fulfilment of arcadian anarchism. In post-Freudian utopias more or less indiscriminate sexual relationships are supposed to be a sign of a scientific attitude.[143] In *Brave New World* this attitude is most systematically exploited; individual love is abolished by proper conditioning, while indiscriminate sexual intercourse serves as a welcome opiate for the people.

But sex can only be dealt with in this way when it is considered in a rather superficial manner. Sex as conceived by writers like D. H. Lawrence would remain the main source of social criticism even under the utopian conditions of *Brave New World*. Sex as a quasi-religious force can give rise to a semi-utopian creation like *The Plumed Serpent* or to a utopia like *Seven Days in New Crete* by Robert Graves (1949). When the social organization has become completely artificial and unnatural, the sexual act itself becomes a symbol of revolt since it is a sign of irrepressible life which may ultimately be victorious over the scientific inhuman social mechanism.

Winston Smith to Julia:

> '"You like doing this? I don't mean simply me: I mean the thing in itself?"
> "I adore it."
> That was above all what he wanted to hear. Not merely the love of one person but the animal instinct, the simple undifferentiated desire that was the force that would tear the Party to pieces. . . . Their embrace had been a battle, the climax a victory. It was a blow struck against the Party. It was a political act.'[144]

Because of this desire, Winston keeps believing that there is hope in the proles. But even here fear of scientific omnipotence steps in.

> 'The sex instinct will be eradicated . . . We shall abolish the orgasm. Our neurologists are at work upon it now . . . There will be no curiosity, no enjoyment of the process of life.'[145]

Instead of the state being shaped for the individual, there the individual will be truly shaped for the state. Each 'man' and 'woman' becomes a perfectly neutral social unit. The long struggle for the equality of the sexes, which has been treated in so many utopian forecasts, has come to a depressing end.[146]

But this is not yet the end of the development towards utopian perversion. First the utopian state secures the happiness of man. Then, the original aim being dropped, propaganda and conditioning secure the stability of the state. Now a final stage of perversion is achieved: the utopian state serves to secure the absolute validity of propaganda; the main function of the state consists in proving that propaganda is truth. In *1984* propaganda has become absolute, truth relative. Formerly utopian propagandists tried to prove that certain false statements were true; now they maintain that there is no such thing as a true or a false statement. Consequently there are no longer propagandists and victims of propaganda; there is only a comprehensive system of 'doublethink', the perverse perfection of the utopian tendency towards stability.

> 'Who controls the past controls the future: who controls the present controls the past.'[147]
> 'The command of the totalitarians was "Thou shalt". Our command is "Thou art".'[148]

As a consequence of 'doublethink' and the systematic annihilation of the documented past there is only one time dimension: the present.

There is no way of thinking beyond what is; therefore what is is absolute. There is no way out of the utopian state, even in thought. In order to make 'doublethink' more effective and in the end inescapable the language is reduced to Newspeak.

> 'The purpose of Newspeak was not only to provide a medium of expression for the world-views and mental habits proper to the devotees of Ingsoc, but to make all other modes of thought impossible.'[149]

The Declaration of Independence for example cannot properly be translated into Newspeak.

> 'A full translation could only be an ideological translation, whereby Jefferson's words would be changed into a panegyric on absolute government.'[150]

So man is first emptied by the processes of technical mass civilization, then he is still further stripped of individuality by propaganda and conditioning of every description. Even torture of the most scientific kind may be applied.

> 'Never again will you be capable of ordinary human feeling. Everything will be dead inside you. Never again will you be capable of love, or friendship, or joy of living, or laughter, or curiosity, or courage, or integrity. You will be hollow. We shall squeeze you empty, and then we shall fill you with ourselves.'[151]

The individual ceases to exist, he is filled with the party, the state. It does not matter much what kind of state it is as far as the social cell is concerned, for in every case the state is the supreme good. Terms like individual happiness or unhappiness cease to have any meaning because there is no longer any standard by which such happiness could be measured. The only happiness possible is the consciousness of serving the state.

Such modern scientific utopias are organized like an army.[152] Like an army they suppress the very idea of revolt. Revolt is even less likely if it can be shown that the utopian organization has the same justification as the army. The most rigorous system will be accepted by the citizens if it is not mere tyranny but the result of self-defence. The most effective means to secure strict adherence to the system is fear, not fear of the system, but fear of some outside force. If this fear is strong enough the feeling generated in the citizen towards the rigorous system will be one of love, love for its protector.

This can fairly easily be achieved if the utopia is restricted to the national scale. In Plato's or More's time this was the only conceivable possibility. All these utopias were prepared for war. In Plato's *Republic* the army was one of the three ranks. More solves the problem with mercenaries. In many cases the problem of war is avoided by placing utopia in some inaccessible island. Or there may be arcadian peace as in Morris's *News from Nowhere*. But generally the idea of war remains important in the utopian imagination. With the development of modern scientific weapons and the increasing danger of global wars the preoccupation with war becomes obsessive. These utopian wars are partly thrillers, partly cautionary tales. Between 1900 and 1914, for instance, there were dozens of the most blood-curdling imaginary invasions of England by the Germans.[153] When war broke out these productions stopped abruptly, only to be followed by a few invasions of the U.S.A.[154]

Before the second world war the situation was different. It seems as if Fascism and Nazism had a special appeal for the British sense of humour, for during the thirties and forties utopian satires on modern dictatorship became very frequent. In most of them we find some absurd megalomaniac together with an abundance of uniformly coloured shirts.[155] Imaginary invasions did not become numerous until later.[156]

Very often such imaginary wars produce a complete collapse of *homo sapiens*. The vision of a relapse into barbarism is another utopian form typical of the twentieth century. Wells's *War in the Air* marks only the beginning of a long tradition.[157] There are a great number of such books in which humanity is reduced to an extremely low level of primitive civilization. These pictures of fallen humanity, of its ignorance, superstitions, fears, and savage violence are usually more impressive than the wars themselves. All are sad tales of civilization lost and science destroyed. They often manage admirably to convey the sense of immense loss. Humanity is groping in the dark, full of faint memories of a former glorious world. Some thousands of years after the downfall of civilization, the drummer is turning the wheel that points to the victim who is to be sacrificed to the powers of darkness. That a wheel might be used for other purposes has been forgotten. It only remains as a symbol of past civilization.

> 'Awana! Awana! Awana! Children of the circles and the wheels that once were, and of the voices that once called across all the jungles, remember.

All (In chorus, mournfully): Awana! We remember.
The Drummer: Once we could cross the hills like the birds of the air.
All: (The same)
The Drummer: Once we could speak, and our voices were loud to the ends of the earth on the wings of our magic.
All: (the same)
The Drummer: Once we could run with our wheels more swiftly than birds can fly or the seekers of meat can spring.
All: (the same)
The Drummer: Awana! Our wheels are broken, and we give of our men and our women to the seekers of meat so that they leave us in peace to the care of our crops.
All: Awana! Our wheels are broken.
The Drummer: We could shoot our arrows with the sound of thunder and none could withstand them; we were the masters and the lords of all that flew in the air, or ran on the earth, or swam in the waters under the earth.
All (wailing): We remember the glory and the power.
The Drummer: We were the lords of creation.
All: We remember the glory and the power.
The Drummer (spinning the wheel faster): Turn, oh wheel, and remind us of the glory and the power.'[158]

This is only one of a great number of similar imaginings in other books. With the arrival of the atomic bomb the theme was further developed in Aldous Huxley's *Ape and Essence*. Here man is reduced to the animal level in the sexual sphere. Human love has become the seasonal outburst of procreating lust. Belial, the god of evil, the god of destructive wars, is worshipped as the most powerful being.[159] Fear of the horrors of a modern war, fear of unspeakable cruelties committed by the conquering enemy, fear of the collapse of civilization are expressed over and over again in recent utopian writing. Abysmal fear and anxiety are the background against which some of the modern regimental utopias must be seen. In J. D. Beresford's *The Riddle of the Tower* (1942) the reduction of humanity takes the shape of an hysterical underworld people, burrowing ever deeper away from the dangerous surface. In Joseph O'Neill's *Land under England* (1935) human beings have become automata devoid of wills and souls. The greater the threatening evil, the more desperate the remedies will be. For all absolutist utopias the *1984* slogan 'War is Peace' is therefore perfectly justified. War, or the fear of war, secures inward peace. The state appears as a benevolent force protecting the citizen against unimaginable horrors. The individual is crushed by the state and gladly accepts total defeat because resistance has been undermined by fear. In *1984* fear and hate of the threatening enemy are the conditions for the unconditional surrender of the individual. The final reconciliation in Winston Smith's mind takes place when he hears of a victory which is probably only a propaganda coup.

> 'He gazed up at the enormous face. Forty years it had taken him to learn what kind of smile was hidden beneath the dark moustache. O cruel, needless misunderstanding! O stubborn, self-willed exile from the loving breast! Two gin-scented tears trickled down the sides of his nose. But it was all right, everything was all right, the struggle was finished. He had won the victory over himself. He loved Big Brother.[160]'

If the individual is not swept away by the dynamic force of collective fear, as in *1984*, he is mass-conditioned to the static tranquillity of collective happiness, as in *Brave New World*. There is not much room for optimistic modern utopias.

In both the long-range evolutionary and the short-range social forecast, utopianism takes the place of traditional religion. In the first case the idea of some future superhuman mankind is the inspiring ideal, in the second it is the idea of the community. Both represent Collective Man. But in the first case the idea can hardly be imaginatively grasped. The ultimate good remains in the future as an inspiring ideal. Where it is pictured, this is only done in a symbolic way; the living reality is still left to the reader's imagination. The social utopias on the other hand describe and imagine an achieved reality. The presentation is realistic rather than allegorical and obviously fantastic. The created picture approximately presents the final stage. By being imaginatively realized the ideal by necessity ceases to be ideal. The imagination of man and his longing for perfection are frustrated. The result is dissatisfaction, even in the case of the misty arcadian anarchies. When, in order to be plausible and convincing, the attained perfection must be concentrated in the admirable functioning of the state, the resulting dissatisfaction is particularly intense. Not only does the state not represent any ulterior ideal but the possible happiness and freedom shared out to its citizens must appear so limited as to make the complex organization meaningless. This may explain the intense malaise in contemporary utopian writing.

'Then an Israeli Sophocrat named ben-Yeshu wrote a book, *A Critique of Utopias*, that greatly impressed his colleagues in Southern Europe, America and Africa. From a detailed and learned analysis of some seventy Utopias, including Plato's *Timaeus* and *Republic*, Bacon's *New Atlantis*, Campanella's *Civitas Solis*, Fénelon's *Voyage en Solente*, Cabet's *Voyage en Icarie*, Lytton's *Coming Race*, Morris's *News from Nowhere*, Butler's *Erewhon*, Huxley's *Brave New World* and various works of the twenty-first to the twenty-fourth centuries, he traced the history of man's increasing discontent with civilization as it developed and came to a practical conclusion: that "we must retrace our steps or perish".'[161]

Part Three

AESTHETIC CONCRETION

I

UTOPIAN FANTASY

LIFE in the future haunts the utopian's mind in many different ways. It affords the subject-matter for various kinds of speculation on human destiny, but it also gives rise to a new kind of grammatical statement. In a utopia the narrator first jumps forward into the future in order to be able to look back at the present. This process enables the writer to use the 'prophetic past',[162] for he is not content with merely looking forwards and speaking in the future tense or the conditional, although from time to time such semi-utopias as Julian Huxley's *If I were Dictator* (1936) make their appearance. A description of a non-existent social system in the future tense or in the conditional would not only be rather clumsy and dull, but the reader would also feel tempted to question the conclusions arrived at. Such conditional statements seem to ask for a refutation since their very grammatical form points to the unreality of the conception in every sentence. Therefore the real utopian is not satisfied unless he can speak of merely possible events which could only take place in the future as if they had really happened.

> 'Pretend that you believe this, and that the following is an authentic message from the Last Men. . . . Otherwise I cannot give life to the great history which it is my task to tell.'[163]

When considering the translation of the evolutionary hypothesis into detailed descriptive accounts of the superman we have seen that the utopian writer works with the desire to transform mere abstract ideas into myths. He tries to work on the readers' imagination in a more powerful and direct way than by arguments and discussions. While the mythical imagination of the evolutionary utopias tends towards the grand scale, the more numerous social utopias are mainly concerned with practical details. Their didactic intent may be more obvious, since it is not their function to provide a sweeping religious view supporting man in his universe. The socially constructive utopias try to convince us how happy we all should be under utopian conditions, which are supposed to be within the reach of present man. After reading an optimistic evolutionary utopia the reader should feel thoroughly satisfied with the lot of mankind in this universe; after reading an optimistically constructive utopia, whether by More, Morris, or Wells, he should on the contrary be thoroughly dissatisfied with the present state of society.

The alluring utopian picture is presented with a considerable quantity of details; but the details of the utopian writer are not the details of the scientific economist. The utopian does not attempt to prove his thesis by long calculations and statistical estimates. In theory his ideas may be rather sweeping, but his utopia is worked out concretely in *suggestive* detail. His imaginary society seems to be alive, and we are actually made to feel what it would be like to live in such a utopia. This pronounced ability to visualize and actualize non-existent conditions also forms the starting point for anti-utopian writing, which may succeed in convincing us that certain plans are not desirable when put into practice, while they may look all right when worked out in the abstract.

The good utopian writer's aim is not limited to the creation of single, disconnected details. Generally he is much more interested in consistently working out a fundamental hypothesis, first giving it imaginative reality and then following it through all its ramifications. Very often, even if it means pushing the initial datum to the most surprising, yet consistent conclusions, the pleasure of seeing a hypothesis realized in all its significant imaginative details is more important to the utopian writer than pursuing his ideals and didactic purpose in real earnest. It is one of the most characteristic aspects of the utopian imagination that it is unlimited. It takes its start in the realm of ideas, then it creates a concrete world of its own, ever extending its view till it is lost in infinity, where man, godlike and immortal, jumps from stellar system to stellar system. On the other hand it keeps narrowing its view, until it arrives at a minute fact. This tendency is clearly expressed in *Utopia* itself. Its communist working society is opposed to capitalism. One of the most obvious consequences of this initial postulate consists in the depreciation of gold and finery. This idea is worked out in picturesque detail when the foreign ambassadors in all their pomp and glory arrive in Utopia, and it finds its fitting consummation in the grotesque, but logical institution of the symbolical gold chamber pots. This line is further pursued in the clothes of the priests, which should be rare and fine, but

> 'theire vestimentes be neither embraudered with gold, nor set with precious stones. But they be wrought so fynely and conningelye

> with divers fethers of foules, that the estimation of no costely stuffe is hable to countervaile the price of the worke.'[164]

The utopian writer delights in ingenuity and seems to write with his tongue in his cheek, sometimes even indulging in laughter.

> 'I laughed when writing both it [*Mr. Blettsworthy on Rampole Island*] and *Men Like Gods* and *The Autocracy of Mr. Parham*.'[165]

Sometimes this delight in amusing ingenuity for its own sake almost entirely dominates a great part of a book, as in Samuel Butler's *Book of the Machines*, on which the author throws some light that may help to illuminate this method in general.

> 'I refer to the chapter upon machines in which I have developed the obviously absurd theory that they are about to supplant the human race and be developed into a higher kind of life. When I first got hold of the idea, *I developed it for mere fun* and because it amused me and I thought would amuse others, but without a particle of serious meaning; but I developed it and introduced it into Erewhon with the intention of implying: "See how easy it is to be plausible, and what absurd propositions can be defended by a little ingenuity and distortion and departure from strictly scientific methods," and I had Butler's *Analogy* in my head as the book at which it should be aimed, but preferred to conceal my aim for many reasons. Firstly, the book was already as heavily weighted with heterodoxy as it would bear, and I dared not give another half ounce lest it should break the camel's back; secondly *it would have interfered with the plausibility of the argument*, and I looked to this *plausibility as a valuable aid to the general acceptation of the book*; thirdly, *it is more amusing* without any sort of explanation, and I thought the drier part that had gone before wanted a little relieving; and also *the more enigmatic a thing of this sort is, the more people think for themselves about it*.'[166]

A utopian writer need not be confined to didacticism. He should not merely be seen as always carefully constructing his new universe because he has come to the conclusion that the best way to reach his audience is to write a utopian tale. Nor is he restricted to cleverly playing with puzzling plausibilities. Even a utopian writer may be moved by a sudden imaginative flash.

> 'And looking up, I saw grey with distance, but still seemingly immense in altitude, the tower of the Waterworks close to the

> street where I was born. It suddenly occurred to me that capturing the Waterworks might really mean the military stroke of flooding the valley; and with that torrent and cataract of visionary waters, the first fantastic notion of a tale called "The Napoleon of Notting Hill" rushed over my mind.'[167]

This is not very surprising in a writer of utopian allegorical fantasies, but even in a minor writer of a scientific utopia the same forces may be at work.

> 'At that time I did not care a great deal for the early scientific novels of H. G. Wells. I was primarily interested in people and in human problems, and not particularly in physical and chemical romance of the Jules Verne school. . . . I had not read any of the scientific romances; neither *The Time Machine* nor *When the Sleeper Awakes* nor *The Country of the Blind.* So it is rather curious that when the idea for my first novel came to me, it should have been a pseudo-scientific utopian one. It occurred to me to wonder what would be the effect on society if the human race could determine in advance the sex of its children. I remember still with complete clarity the time and place where this notion impinged upon my imagination. It gave me an almost physical shock of excitement and pleasure, one of those mysterious shocks experienced by the creative artist at the first moment of impact of an "inspiration".'[168]

But whatever the exact circumstances of the origin of a utopia may be, whatever the exact mixture of its amusing, puzzling, or didactic components, the desire for the concretion and individualization of a general social idea remains the most important factor. While the reader's attention is fixed on the utopian narrative, the events and facts have to be accepted, surprising as they may be. If the reader refuses this suspension of disbelief he cannot enjoy the story. But the writer has to help the reader along towards such a state of suspension of disbelief. Presenting the non-existent as if it really existed in merely grammatical form does not do away with all difficulties. The question of reality enters by another door. Will not the whole utopian picture appear so obviously untrue, that the desire for concreteness defeats its own ends?

In principle the creation of an imaginary state may be considered the same as the creation of a fictitious character, but it is by no means the same in scale and degree. Inventing a few persons that never existed may evoke hardly any sceptical comment from the reader. He is in no position to prove that they actually do not exist since it would be extremely difficult for him to check their identities among the many millions of other individuals. The facts are not materially altered. So it is not surprising that a good many naïve readers hardly distinguish between fictitious and real people. But even if a novel is preceded by a statement that all the characters are fictitious, they are generally such as might easily exist according to our common knowledge. Documentary evidence does not play an important part in such cases. It is not a question of what is real, but of what corresponds to our notions of reality, of what is natural in the widest sense of the word. With the creation of an imaginary state the case is different, for here there is hardly any danger of confusing the real and the fictitious. By inventing a non-existent state the author deviates from well-known facts, may even depart from natural laws. He enters a new domain with quite special aspects and different interests: the realm of the fantastic.

> 'What does fantasy ask of us? It asks us to pay something extra. It compels us to an additional adjustment. The other novelists say "Here is something that might occur in your lives", the fantasist "Here is something that could not occur".'[169]

But even in such utopian fantasy there are degrees, and the utopian device, which is included among the time-honoured fantastic means by Mr. Forster, sometimes merges with the more usual novel. Fictitious names of counties and towns do not in the least interfere with realism. Even simply inventing a new name for a country does not yet make a novel fantastic or utopian, although the country does not exist on the map. But with the invention of new names for whole countries realism generally begins to recede. Such countries as Ruritania, Balkania, Azania mostly represent typified abstracted local colour. They are vaguely situated in the Balkans, in Africa, or among the South American republics. Such countries are specially adapted to this purpose because they belong to a group of similar ones. Like Evelyn Waugh's *Black Mischief*, novels making use of such states are generally slightly irresponsible, operatic products rather than wildly fantastic ones. Names of particular well-defined states like the U.S.A., England, or Russia are hardly changed that way. Sometimes the newly created exotic and romantic countries may be used, as are Lilliput and Erewhon, to satirize a country which does not belong to the group originally designated. So the small pseudo-German kingdom in Laurence Housman's Jingalo stories satirizes English institutions and stands somewhere between Ruritania and Erewhon. This is one among many possible variations.

As long as the nature of the country, whose name or geographical existence is unknown or plainly non-existent, conforms to our notions of what a country in those parts of the world would be like, its existence can be accepted by the reader as a matter of course. But as soon as these conditions are not fulfilled, as soon as the nature of the country, its inhabitants and civilization contradict the reader's prejudices, it becomes fantastic. A white tribe in the middle of the African continent or a highly mechanized and advanced society on an island in the Pacific are fantastic, possibly utopian, if social criticism is involved. The utopian creations tend to be fantastic because their civilizations are so unheard of that they cannot be placed anywhere on earth without being wildly incongruous; while, as soon as they are placed among the stars or in the future, they become even more fantastic, because they are out of our reach of knowledge. Only arcadian utopias stressing the return to nature may seem fairly plausible and in accordance with conditions in certain parts of the world, or at least with their idealized images in the eyes of western man. At first the utopian hypothesis is, as it were, in the air. Then it becomes more solid when realized in the description of the utopian state. But the utopian state itself still remains in the air.

The attempt to connect such fantastic states with reality may be explained as the final outcome of the utopian's desire to create the illusion of reality. Again it is not only the desire for a greater impact on the reader's mind that moves the author. The existence of the utopian state is also a challenge to his ingenuity, to his imagination which cannot be stopped; it amuses him to puzzle out the connection between the hypothesis and everyday reality. For the utopian it would never do to place a hard and factual state in some vague and shadowy world. The account has to be of the same concrete quality throughout. Therefore he invents the *journey to utopia*.—Hand in hand with the desire for concreteness there goes the desire for actualization. The one preceeds from the hypothesis to the description of the hypothetical state, and finally to explaining away its hypothetical nature. The other proceeds from the hypothesis to description, thence to narrative, trying to present the utopian state not only in the most concrete, but also in the most dramatic way. This need for action was expressed at the very beginning of utopian writing by Socrates in *Timaeus*:

> 'Then I may now proceed to tell you how I feel about the society we have just described [The Republic]. My feelings are much like those of a man who has beheld superb animals in a drawing, or, it may be, in real life, but at rest, and finds himself longing to

> behold them in motion, executing some feat commensurate with their physique. That is just how I feel about the city we have described.'[170]

In this remark the later development of the utopian imaginary historical account is foreshadowed, but the journey to utopia generally serves the same purpose. The utopian traveller's mind reflects the impact of a strange society with greater force by his reactions, which may even lead to a dramatic conflict. Both the desire for greater verisimilitude and for greater dramatization make the utopian journey a useful and well-established device.

If we take a historical rather than a deductive view, we have to consider that the genre of the imaginary journey is even older than the utopian genre. Every imaginary journey or extraordinary journey contains the seeds of a utopian romance, and a utopia could be regarded as a development of such imaginary journeys. In fact, the two join forces; on the one hand the desire for a realistic utopia naturally tends towards the creation of a utopian journey, on the other hand the existence of imaginary journeys makes utopias more easily possible. In certain cases the first circumstance predominates, in others the second. In More's case the creation of utopia preceded the journey and the geographical setting. In cases like Godwin's *Man in the Moon* (1638) and many modern scientific romances it is the utopian element which is the by-product. The extremely varied literary traditions which can be at work in a single piece of utopian writing have been traced and analysed through *Gulliver's Travels* in Eddy's critical study.[171] This work furnishes a striking proof that the origins of utopian writing are multiple and cannot be reduced to a single element.

Is the journey to utopia meant to be taken literally or is it to be considered a clever hoax? What is its position between the extremes of realism and fantasy?

The original technique of introducing utopia is exemplified in Plato's *Critias*, More's *Utopia*, Bacon's *New Atlantis*, Swift's *Gulliver's Travels*, Butler's *Erewhon*, Wells's *Time Machine* and many others. The reader's reaction in all these cases ought to be similar to that elicited from the listeners in *New Atlantis*: 'for indeed we were all astonished to hear so strange things so probably told'.[172] The method employed may be called the technique of fantastic realism.

All utopian voyages are either fantastic or at the least extraordinary. There have been attempts to classify such imaginary voyages as 'realistic' on the one hand, and 'fantastic' on the other.[173] This does not seem to lead very far and is essentially confusing. After having defined a 'realistic' voyage as one 'to an existing country, or one that might easily exist, in which the mode of travel and the adventures are restricted to the possibilities of an actual voyage', Eddy continues:

> 'In determining the "possibilities of an actual voyage" the knowledge possessed by the author's contemporaries must be taken into account. A seventeenth century voyage describing unicorns and hermaphrodites does not on that account fail to be a Realistic Voyage however prodigious such features may seem to the modern scientist.'[174]

If descriptions of unicorns and hermaphrodites are realistic why should this term not be extended till it ceases to have any meaning? Why should supernatural and magical interference be excluded when dealing with the seventeenth century? The subject-matter, the plain facts as they would emerge in a short summary of such a journey may be more or less credible, fantastic or realistic, but here it is wiser to abstain from using such terms as 'realistic' or 'fantastic'. In Eddy's terms all journeys to the moon would have to be classed as fantastic, while most of the discoveries on earth would be realistic. Such a definition might possibly be accepted for the sixteenth, seventeenth, and even the eighteenth century. But since in considering such journeys one has to take into account the nature of travelling as well as the nature of the imaginary country this distinction breaks down when applied under modern conditions. For nowadays the more credible and ordinary the means of travel the more incredible the existence of the unknown country will be. A journey into the African interior may be very plausible, but because of its very plausibility and ordinariness the discovery of an unknown utopian country in regions which have been explored is all the more extraordinary and fantastic. In order to be acceptable a modern utopia will have to be placed in unknown regions outside the earthly sphere. But in such a case the mode of travel presents much greater difficulties. So the utopian creations all tend to be fantastic in a merely factual sense. Once the transition to the unknown country has been achieved, the creatures inhabiting those parts may take all kinds of shapes and adopt the most unusual customs, for there is no *a priori* natural law prohibiting the existence of unicorns and hermaphrodites, or anarchy and antlike regimentation.

The distinction between realistic and fantastic utopian journeys according to mode of travel and the nature of the destination is not satisfactory. On the whole a utopian journey is fantastic. But another aspect is much more interesting and illuminating: that is the narrative treatment of such journeys. From the point of view of the narrative method a journey to the moon can be realistic or fantastic. The subject-matter itself being fantastic one may distinguish between realistic and plain fantasy. According to Herbert Read the two necessary attributes of plain or pure fantasy are objectivity and arbitrariness. On both counts he raises objections against utopias:

> 'A "Utopia", or description of a fantastical country and its civilization, might well exhibit all the characteristics of pure Fantasy, but rarely does so because the writer has some ulterior satirical or moral aim, which aim distorts his composition, fixes it in space and time, gives it a basis of subjective intolerance. Such objections apply to *Utopia* itself, to *News from Nowhere* and *The Dream of John Ball*, to *Erewhon* and *A Crystal Age*. They do not apply to some of the fantasies of H. G. Wells, who comes as near as any modern writer to a sense of pure fantasy. He errs, as in *The Time Machine*, by imparting to his fantasies a pseudo-scientific logicality; it is as though having conceived an arbitrary fantasy he were compelled by the habits of his scientific training to work out the consequences of this fantasy. Real fantasy is bolder than this; it dispenses with all logic and habit, and relies on the force of wonder alone.'[175]

It is not surprising that a utopia cannot be pure fantasy because of its lack of objectivity and arbitrariness. An 'objective' utopia, i.e. an imaginary country whose institutions are not related to its time and which has no moral significance is by definition not a utopia, but only a fantastical country. Lack of arbitrariness, on the other hand, is not a necessary condition of utopian writing, and here we are specially concerned with this aspect. In Wells's fantasies this arbitrariness is said to be impaired by a 'pseudo-scientific logicality'. This tendency makes Wells's fantasies realistic fantasies, his method fantastic realism. Herbert Read does not consider the other utopias with regard to arbitrariness, but some of them exhibit the same pseudo-scientific logicality. This is not simply a matter of scientific training, but of the utopian type of mind which takes pleasure in working things out logically, proceeding from hypothetical premises to detailed concrete conclusions. The utopian does not even aim at arbitrariness; on the contrary, he tries to avoid it, striving to construct a coherent pseudo-logical reality. The irony implied in the use of such a device corresponds to the utopian's consciousness of the gap between appearance and reality which he tries to bridge. In purely fantastic writing reality simply recedes. The fairy tale simply states: 'Once upon a time . . .' and the reader can take it or leave it. No affirmations or claims of veracity are made. The attitude expressed is truly naïve. In utopian writing there is always a double level, the implication being: 'Here in this really existing utopia things are like this; they could also be like this in our known reality, but of course they are not, and perhaps, after all, they could not really be so, for we know, don't we, that this utopia does not really exist.' The fantastic realist protests that he deals with realities, but he does so with his tongue in his cheek; he is highly sophisticated and self-conscious; he is acutely aware that there are statements which do not correspond to events, that the word and the thing are not the same, and that there is the possibility of fiction, of 'saying the thing which is not'.

2

IRONICAL REALISM

THIS sophisticated self-consciousness is clearly demonstrated by the writer's protestations of truth, which are meant to ensure a superficial verisimilitude as well as a deeper ironical effect. The writer confesses that he has to relate a most extraordinary tale, but that the events nevertheless really did happen. This is the first and oldest device of fantastic realism. It achieved such an early popularity that it afforded a subject of sufficient importance for Lucian's satirical attack in the *True History*:

> 'Many other writers have adopted the same plan, professing to relate their own travels, and describing monstrous beasts, savages, and strange ways of life. . . . When I come across a writer of this sort, I do not so much mind his lying; . . . I am only surprised at his expecting to escape detection.'[176]

The method had some effect on the more naïve kind of reader, and it has been employed again and again.

> 'Therefore since my Acquaintances were pleased to think my poor Endeavours might not be unacceptable to my Country, I imposed on myself as a Maxim never to be swerved from, that I would *strictly adhere to Truth*.'[177]
>
> 'My chief consolation lies in the fact that truth bears its own impress, and that my story will carry conviction by reason of the internal evidences for its accuracy. No one who is himself honest will doubt my being so.'[178]

Similar protestations have been used by More in even subtler ways, especially in the attached Letter to Peter Giles. There the truth of the account is not blatantly announced, but emerges unobtrusively in a discussion of style. New twists and turns of this age-old technique are always being invented; sometimes a minor author may hit on a most effective and comical version. Such is the case in Eimar O'Duffy's *Spacious Adventures of the Man in the Street* (1928). The unfortunate Dubliner whose astral body has been conjured out of his earthly body, travels to foreign stars, much against his will. On his return to earth he discovers that he has lost his job, through no fault of his own. He indites a letter of justification to his manager, protesting that he could not help what had happened to him. It is with this letter that the story begins: 'Honestly, Mr. Gallagher!' This is one of the most amusing utopian introductions, but unfortunately, as in so many other cases, the invention is not sustained and flags when the traveller gets to utopia.

As Lucian points out in the passage cited above, a part of this technique consists in relating one's own travels. All such imaginary journeys have the nature of reports, usually written in the first person singular. The narrative in the first person is meant to give an even more convincing air of authenticity and verisimilitude, providing undoubted first-hand information.

> 'It has hitherto been supposed that the four men who were in the dinghy perished, but this is incorrect: I have the best evidence for this assertion—I am one of the four men. . . .'[179]

Preferably the hero's circumstances are expounded at some length. In More's *Utopia* we are told a great deal about Hythloday's personal history and we are also accurately informed about Gulliver's antecedents. This obvious and generally used technique of spurious genealogy and personal history was early satirized in Samuel Brunt's *Voyage to Cacklogallinia* (1727), and later Samuel Butler rejected it in the very first words of *Erewhon* because it seemed a rather stale and clumsy device:

> 'If the reader will excuse me, I will say nothing of my antecedents, nor of the circumstances which led me to leave my native country; the narrative would be tedious to him and painful to myself.'[180]

But the report in the first person singular is all the same very firmly established in utopian fiction, sometimes producing very strange results indeed, as in W. H. Hudson's *A Crystal Age* (1887). This story is told as if the narrator were sitting comfortably in an arm-chair relating past adventures at ease. Towards the end of the story the narrator's consciousness fades out completely in a death which takes place a few thousand years hence. In order to make some sense the whole story would have to be thought of as an instantaneous compression of the hero's last thoughts. But this effect is not aimed at. As it is, the narrative in the first person leaves the reader completely bewildered, because a new theme—the hero's death in utopia—and an old technique, do not coalesce. In *The Green Child* Herbert Read deals with a similar theme in the third person, without the least complication of narrative technique. On the whole the utopian narrative in the first person recedes in importance in the twentieth century. Nineteenth-century utopians like Bulwer, Butler, Bellamy, Hudson, and Morris all use the first person. Wells employs it sometimes, but most modern writers do not rely on it any longer.[181]

When employing the technique of ironical realism the writer does not rely on the slender claim of the first person alone, but tries to provide further circumstantial evidence, documents, official authorities. As was clearly demonstrated by the legendary invasion from Mars in 1938 this method can really take effect where the naïve mind is concerned.

> 'I believed the broadcast as soon as I heard the professor from Princeton and the officials in Washington.'
> 'I knew it was an awfully dangerous situation when all those military men were there and the Secretary of State spoke.'
> 'If so many of those astronomers saw the explosions they must have been real. They ought to know.' etc.[182]

A great part of the pleasure derived from reading such books consists in reading them at a double level, in continuously imagining such a naïve reader who is taken in by these devices. In order to achieve such deception, certain barriers restricting ordinary fiction may be broken down. The utopian narrative is not only presented as a documentary report, but even as a pamphlet inciting the reader to take immediate action. So there is no doubt at all that the utopian account is very much part of everyday reality on the newspaper level.

> 'Please subscribe quickly. Address to the Mansion-House, care of the Lord Mayor whom I will instruct to receive names and subscriptions for me until I can organize a committee.'[183]

All these means, protestations of truth, first person, and documentary evidence, are part of an assertive method which tries to convince the reader that black is white by saying so very loudly and repeating it over and over again. Fantastic realism does not rely on this method alone, but combines it with the evasive method, which leads the reader away from the well-known into the regions of uncertainty.

This evasive method shows itself most clearly when the author locates his imaginary country. As we have seen, the location of the imaginary state is the more plausible, the less we can disprove its existence. Only it must not be completely out of the reach of human means of travel. In former times, when there was enough room left for further geographical discoveries, the task of finding an appropriate location for the utopian country was none too difficult.

> 'Swift's primary geographical problem was not a difficult one. He had to find in the unexplored portions of the globe, locations for seven imaginary countries, only two of which were of considerable size. It was desirable that these locations should not be so close to either pole as to be obviously unfit for human habitation, and Swift apparently felt also that they should not be too close to the equator, the climates do not seem to differ much from that of England. It was also necessary to take care that these countries did not lie too close to each other, or to trade routes generally known to Europeans, though on the other hand, they could not lie too far from these routes, lest it should be difficult to account for Gulliver's arrivals and departures.'[184]

Such were the main principles guiding the early utopian writer and such were the difficulties besetting his path in this respect. Detailed maps, indications of longitude and latitude, and accurate descriptions of the course pursued as used in *Gulliver's Travels* were the best means of creating the impression of a true report. But since this method ceased to work, as it became easier and easier to disprove the existence of the imaginary country, a more effective and radical method of evasion had to be adopted.

Utopia itself leads the way. In spite of the very detailed and accurate description of the extent and organization of the country, the geographical location is vague. Some few data are provided, but they only serve to confuse the reader further. We hear about the Macariens, 'which be not far distant from Utopia', about the Zapoletes who live 500 miles east of Utopia, and about the Achoriens, 'which be situate over against the Island of Utopia on the south-east side.' We only know that Utopia is somewhere south of the tropics. This unsatisfactory vagueness, conflicting with the general technique of utopian realism in More's work, is explained in Peter Giles' Letter:

> 'For, as touchinge the situation of the ylande, that is to saye, in what parte of the worlde Utopia standeth, the ignoraunce and lacke whereof not a little troubleth and greveth master More, in dede Raphael left not that unspoken of. Howbeit with verie fewe wordes he lightly touched it, incidentlye by the way passing it over, as meaning of likelihod to kepe and reserve that to an other place. And the same, I wot not know, by a certain evell and unluckie chaunce escaped us bothe. For when Raphael was speaking therof, one of Master Mores servauntes came to him and whispered in his eare. Wherefore I beyng then of purpose more earnestly addict to heare, one of the company, by reason of cold taken, I thinke, a shippeborde, coghed out so loude, that he toke from my hearinge certen of his wordes. But I wil never stynte, nor rest until I have gotte the full and exacte knowledge hereof.'[185]

The fantastic realist never ceases to worry ironically about the most inconsiderable details. The technique remains the same no matter how much the actual mode of travel may have developed from sailing ship to spaceship. In most seventeenth and eighteenth-century voyages some convenient storm and shipwreck interferes with navigation and provides the plausible evasion, but in more modern times this device has ceased to be popular and a more psychological and at the same time simpler method has been discovered. Bulwer-Lytton in *The Coming Race* at first seems to evade the claims of accuracy by the clumsy use of blanks and dashes. But suddenly this apparent disadvantage is turned into an asset:

> 'The reader will understand, ere he close this narrative, my reason for concealing all clue to the district of which I write, and will perhaps thank me for refraining from any description that may tend to its discovery.'[186]

The reason is that the rediscovery of the Vril-ya might possibly involve the destruction of our much inferior human race. We do not know this till later, but the mysterious hint suffices to arouse some curiosity and to suggest to the reader the immense actuality of the story which prevents the writer from being more explicit. The implied meaning is that it would be very easy to give a detailed description if it were mere fiction. Samuel Butler uses a very similar procedure, on the one hand insisting on the importance of his discovery, on the other hand concealing its location for prudential reasons:

> 'I fear that my story will be doubted unless I tell the whole of it, and yet I dare not do so, lest others with more means than mine should get the start of me.'[187]

This method of evasion is continued in modern utopian fiction, e.g. Viscount Samuel's *An Unknown Land*; but generally fantastic realism undergoes still further changes in modern times, partly because of the ingenuity of the authors, partly because of the ever increasing demands arising from the expansion of knowledge. While in former ages it was quite natural to assume the existence of living beings on the moon since it seemed a place sufficiently protected against any danger of verification, a modern writer has to overcome difficulties which Francis Godwin, Defoe or Samuel Brunt did not and could not imagine.[188] In Wells's *First Men in the Moon* the prospective utopian travellers cannot discover any traces of life on the moon by telescope and they come to the conclusion that there cannot be any life, all the more because the natural conditions are not suitable. So, quite obviously, if there is to be any life at all, it has to be placed inside the moon, where it is adequately protected from the immense cold. This initial idea in its turn gives rise to a whole world of fantastic inventions which make the hypothesis work in every detail.

If the utopian country is placed outside the terrestrial sphere, as happens in many modern utopias, the attention of the fantastic realist is fixed on a plausible means of connecting utopia with our world rather than on evading the question of its exact location. A connection need not be established by means of a journey as long as the knowledge about the imaginary country is satisfactorily accounted for. In the case of Plato's *Atlantis* an old manuscript and oral tradition serve as a means of communication, in Wells's *First Men in the Moon* some of the reports are transmitted by wireless, and in Stapledon's *Last and First Men* an extremely complicated and confusing technique of thought-transmission is employed. But on the whole the two most popular modern connections are the extraterrestrial journey and the time journey.

The first type has a long tradition which has been dealt with by

Marjorie Nicolson.[189] Lucian's truly fabulous extraterrestrial voyages are pure fantasy, while Francis Godwin's *Man in the Moon* (1638) is not only the proper beginning for English journeys to the moon, but also marks the starting point for a new 'scientific' approach, although his science must seem rather primitive in modern eyes. Domingo Gonzales, the hero, is transported to the moon by a number of huge swan-like birds. But these powerful birds are only partly responsible for his strange journey, 'attraction' and 'gravity' being more important than they.

> 'At length, O incredible thing, they forbore moving anything at all, and yet remained unmoveable as stedfastly, as if they had beene upon so many perches; the lines slacked; neither I nor the Engine moved at all, but abode still as having no manner of weight.'[190]

Here flight is easy and swift, and there is no distinction between the different directions: 'upward, downward, or sidelong, all was one'. Other pseudo-scientific techniques are used in Defoe's *Consolidator* or Brunt's *Voyage to Cacklogallinia*, but they are not really plausible. Even Defoe, a master of realistic detail, remains rather vague about the method of propulsion; his machine is fed with 'a certain spirit, deposited in a proper quantity to last out the voyage'.[191] In modern times such vagueness can be justified, if the writer evades awkward questions by relying on the generally known fact that modern science, especially research in physics, has made such tremendous progress that almost anything may seem possible. At the same time it is well-known that the problems involved are extremely complicated and can only be dealt with by a first-rate specialist. Easiest and most plausible is the following course:

> 'For a moment Weston seemed disposed to give no answer; then as if on second thought, he sat down on the bed beside Ransom and spoke as follows: I suppose it will save trouble if I deal with these questions at once, instead of leaving you to pester us with them every hour for the next month. As to how we do it—I suppose you mean how the spaceship works—there is no good your asking that. Unless you were one of the four or five real physicists now living you couldn't understand: and if there were any chance of your understanding you certainly would not be told. If it makes you happy to repeat words that don't mean anything—which is, in fact, what unscientific people mean when they ask for an explana-

> tion—you may say we work by exploiting the less observed properties of solar radiation.'[192]

Of course, there is no answer to this line of argument, but such a very modern plausible refusal to consider and describe the details is not so satisfactory as the more old-fashioned circumstantial method. A detailed explanation is highly effective when presented with sufficient energy and with a considerable amount of pseudo-scientific terms which will leave the reader in a state of resigned bewilderment. The utopian technique has been improved and developed by many modern writers, but in this particular field Wells has not been surpassed. In his *First Men in the Moon*, for instance, the spaceship is made of *Cavorite*. This strange material does not exploit 'the less observed properties of solar radiation', which does not give the reader's mind anything to work on. Cavorite is 'opaque to gravity'. Everyone knows what opaqueness and gravity mean. It is quite simple, and it is equally obvious that the concept is an absurd one. But now the fantastic realist starts working with a torrential stream of pseudo-scientific jargon, using all kinds of spurious arguments and false analogies so that after a while the reader begins to wonder whether there might not be something in it after all. Although he will probably still be convinced that the idea is absurd, he will be incapable of disproving it off-hand, unless he is used to dealing with such arguments. In any case, the reader is not only quite soberly told that there are unsuspected depths in our universe, but he is made to feel it. This is achieved by presenting the fantastic problem in apparently well-known and reliable terms.

> 'The invention is nothing in itself and when this kind of thing is attempted by clumsy writers who do not understand this elementary principle nothing could be conceived more silly and extravagant. Anyone can invent human beings inside out or worlds like dumbbells or a gravitation that repels. The thing that makes such imaginations interesting is their translation into everyday terms.'
> 'For the writer of fantastic stories to help the reader to play the game properly, he must help him in every possible way to domesticate the impossible hypothesis. He must trick him into an unwary concession to some plausible assumption and get on with the story while the illusion holds.'[193]

The same rules apply to the time journey, the most recent type of utopian travelling. Of course one may say that all journeys to utopia are time journeys in disguise. *Utopia* has evolved from something like Tudor England, *The Coming Race* is the evolutionary result of Victorian England, and in *A Modern Utopia* or *An Unknown Land* ideal countries are presented, based on the England of the twentieth century. After the unknown country has been discovered in space the author is free to substitute any level of development he likes. Non-existent space is used to present non-existent time. The journey in space predominated in all the earlier stages of utopian fiction because it seemed to be the only effective means of achieving realistic concreteness in every respect. Apart from creating a spatially co-existent future there remained only the dream and the vision if the writer wanted to transcend the present. But employing such means would have meant a corresponding loss in verisimilitude and concreteness.

> 'Il est étrange que le moyen d'évasion le plus facile et le plus authentique, le rêve, n'ait été utilisé que si tard par les Utopistes.'[194]

After what has been said about the utopian imagination this does not seem so very strange. There does not seem to be much point in presenting a dream as a dream if one is concerned with proving or suggesting its practicability. *News from Nowhere* is practically the only well-known dream utopia.

Because of its greater concreteness the prolonged trancelike sleep proved more popular, especially before the influence of the time machine made itself felt.[195] The hero falls asleep and only wakes up a few hundred years later. So he is bodily transported to utopia. Such prolonged sleep may explain the time journey itself but it cannot be treated in the documentary fashion required by fantastic realism, since there is no way of explaining how the narrative reaches the contemporary reader. In Hudson's case the result borders on the absurd, in Wells's the product is plain fiction, while Bellamy rather ingeniously addresses the contemporary reader as if he were a member of the future generation. But none of them attempts the apparently impossible task of returning into the present. Only the new theories of time and space have made possible fantastically realistic voyages into the future, and Wells's *Time Machine* is the prototype of fantastic realism in modern utopian fiction. *The Time Machine* marked the transition from vague dreamlike time fantasies to hard, scientific treatment. Originally *The Time Machine* had been a rather old-fashioned fantasy, but Wells rewrote it several times till it took its present form. This change affected even the title which had originally been *Chronic Argonauts*.

'And think of 'Chronic' and 'Argonauts' in the title! The ineptitude of this rococo title for a hard mathematical invention.'[196]

Wells himself used other ways as well in order to project the reader into the future. In *Men Like Gods*, for instance, some travellers are hurled into a different system of space-time by utopian experiments, which are carried out in the future. Many post-Wellsian anticipations use similar stream-lined accounts, inventing ever new variations even within such a restricted field.[197] But in spite of the many possible variations, Wells haunts the minds of most modern utopian writers working in the medium of fantastic realism. They try to escape his influence or to outdo him in his own particular domain without being quite convinced of their success. Some even go out of their way to anticipate possible attacks on their supposed lack of originality:

'... the idea of a Time Machine is not new; but as there is a Wellsian precedent for nearly every pseudo-scientific anticipation of the future, the film should not be discredited on that account.'[198]

All these utopian journeys are barometers of the scientific knowledge of the age at a popular level. Scientific ideas are absorbed and reflected imaginatively by the fantastic realist, no matter what the exact nature of the idea may be. Utopian fantastic realism is distinguished from other kinds by its own particular mixture: evolutionary hypothesis, space-time idea, and social construction and criticism.

In order to make the fantastic hypothesis really plausible the assertive and evasive methods have to be supplemented by a general air of realism: by an attention to small details that may have nothing to do with the invention itself. The realistic setting is at least as important as the realistic treatment of the fantastic conception.

'In all this type of story the living interest lies in their non-fantastic elements and not in the invention itself.'

'As soon as the magic trick has been done the whole business of the fantasy writer is to keep everything else human and real. Touches of prosaic detail are imperative and a rigorous adherence to the hypothesis. Any *extra* fantasy outside the cardinal assump-

> tion gives a touch of irresponsible silliness to the invention. So soon as the hypothesis is launched the whole interest becomes the interest of looking at human feelings and human ways, from the new angle that has been acquired.'[199]

Wells insists on the story being human once the fantastic trick has been done. But it has to be human and realistic even before, simply in order that the magic trick can be performed. This principle has been observed very clearly by Plato in *Timaeus*, when creating the setting for the account of Atlantis. Critias' story of Atlantis had been told to him by his grandfather when Critias was hardly more than ten years old. This is in itself not very plausible, since it asks for a prodigious feat of memory. So the bald statement is touched up with realistic details.

> 'How true the saying is that we have a wonderful memory for what we learn in childhood! I hardly know whether I can recollect all I heard yesterday, but I should be much surprised if I have lost a single detail of this story, though it is so very long since it was told me. You see, it gave me a great deal of sport and enjoyment to listen and the old man was delighted to answer my repeated questions; thus it has all been impressed on me like the lines of an indelible design.'[200]

Then this general setting is worked out with details like the following:

> 'The old man—how well I recall the scene—broke into a delighted smile.'[201]

This is the beginning of an elaborate technique of circumstantial detail. Everything that could easily be true is stressed and presented with the greatest possible accuracy so that it seems to be based on actual observation and experience.

> 'The same man . . . did so open and declare the matter, that he might plainely enough appeare, to report not thinges which he had heard of others onelye by heare say, but which he had with his own eyes presently sene, and throughly viewed.'[202]

The main issue becomes obscured, the reader is tied down to plausible details on the narrow path before him so that he hardly notices the surprising changes in the surrounding landscape. Hythloday, Gulliver, and many other early travellers to utopia provide plain and objective information. In the later romances of this kind the use of the traveller's person is extended. Instead of producing a hard and dry objective account, the utopian traveller begins to interpose his consciousness between the utopian facts and the reader. To a certain degree this may be true of Hythloday and Gulliver, but their very emotional reactions are objectified. They may be astonished, surprised, afraid, they may even occasionally vent their feelings, but they largely remain convenient mental yard-sticks or registering machines. They impress by their hard objectivity, but they hardly convey a sense of the utopian atmosphere. Gulliver's body may be threatened by all kinds of dangers, but his mind seems to be soaring outside, calmly observing and measuring all the time. The factual reality of the outside world is portrayed admirably, but the reality of the emotional experience has to be taken more or less for granted. Later utopian writers try to correct this by an impressionistic or atmospheric technique. In More's *Utopia* the qualities of the commonwealth are calmly praised. In *News from Nowhere* and *A Crystal Age* on the other hand there is a feeling of joy and beauty. Gulliver is afraid of the huge Brobdingnagians, but the hero of *The Coming Race* and the Wellsian small man among the future generations are really haunted by a sense of strangeness, of fear, of being absolutely lost. The hypothesis is worked out and the individual's reactions are recorded in vivid detail. If the emotional reactions are transmitted with sufficient intensity the reality of the hypothesis is not directly presented, but can be inferred from the quality of the personal experience. A skilful writer will combine documentary and impressionistic realism. Wells does not spare any pseudo-scientific means at his disposal in order to construct a time machine. But later in the story the time machine becomes real because the time traveller's experience, the feeling of passing through time at terrific speed, is rendered with such striking vividness:

> 'Then in the intermittent darkness, I saw the moon spinning swiftly through her quarters from new to full, and had a faint glimpse of the circling stars. Presently, as I went on, still gaining velocity, the palpitation of night and day merged into continuous greyness; the sky took on a wonderful deepness of blue, a splendid luminous colour like that of twilight; the jerking sun became a streak of fire, a brilliant arch in space; the moon a fainter fluctuating band; and I could see nothing of the stars, save now and then a bright circle flickering in the blue. The landscape was misty and

> vague. I saw trees growing and changing like puffs of vapour: now brown, now green; they grew, spread, shivered, and passed away. I saw huge buildings rise up faint and fair, and pass like dreams. The whole surface of the earth seemed changed—melting and flowing under my eyes. . . . Presently I noted that the sun belt swayed up and down, from solstice to solstice, in a minute or less, and that consequently my pace was over a year a minute; and minute by minute the white snow flashed across the world, and vanished, and was followed by the bright brief green of spring.'[203]

The whole process is rendered as the time traveller's sense experience. The time traveller's mind and body are a unit, a moving point in space and time. The experience seems real, but the concrete external reality recedes; the hard rational outlines are replaced by a blurring rhythm of pointillistic sense data.

The last stage of fantastic realism has been reached. If this impressionistic technique is consistently developed and extended to cover the description of the utopian country it defeats itself. There has been one highly ambitious attempt to apply the stream of consciousness to utopian narrative.[204] This Kinemato-Romance is a failure, for in order to be effective the reality which it reflects has to be presupposed, known and existent. If, as in a utopia, this is not the case, the technique breaks down. The stream of consciousness cannot be properly related to anything, because the utopian reality is an unknown quantity, which has to be created in the book. Consequently the consciousness seems to work in a vacuum. It is almost like a tale told by an idiot who reacts against his own imaginary universe the nature of which must remain a mystery to us.

Psychological impressionism may be very useful from time to time in a utopian narrative, but the traditional utopian writer is on his guard against it. When Mr. Higgs returns from his second visit from Erewhon in *Erewhon Revisited* his mind is gone. This is an effective satirical device, but it forces Butler to change his narrative technique. A direct first person narrative as in *Erewhon*, if coherent, would be implausible; if psychologically realistic, it would deflect the reader's attention from the utopian satire to the hero's madness. Therefore the responsibility for the narrative is shifted to the son, whose task consists in transforming the disjointed utterances of his father into a coherent whole. Thus Butler avoids both dangers of psychological impressionism: the blurring of the utopian picture and the disproportionate importance of the hero.

For these reasons the socially constructive or satirical writer generally restricts the technique of fantastic realism to assertion, evasion, and objective description. He may add occasional impressionistic touches and other means of intensifying the imaginative impact of his story, but if these predominate the writer's aim is very often a different one.

3

SYMBOLICAL JOURNEYS

In the utopian documentary report as well as in pure fantasy the reality of the fantastic occurrence is accepted as something that cannot be doubted. The traveller may be forced to admit that he felt rather surprised or that it all seemed very queer, but he is not essentially disturbed by such admissions. He remains wide awake and at home in the world of solid everyday reality. Psychological realism in utopia goes some way beyond this sense of hard facts. It may still impart the feeling of hard concreteness, but it also stresses the strangeness and inexplicable wonder of the happenings. There is a new openness and receptiveness of mind. The Wellsian traveller may react very violently in action and feelings, but only very rarely does he step over the limits of his curiously registering mind. He may be shocked or frightened, but generally he is not moved by a sense of mystery and a feeling of deeper spiritual significance underlying his extraordinary experiences. The impressions absorbed by him may be intensified to such a degree as to assume a certain nightmarish quality or they may be blurred by a momentary ecstatic stridency, but the hard facts still dominate, nor is it Wells's aim to achieve a different effect. Yet in recent times utopian fantasy has also used other ways and means in order to achieve a deeper penetration. There may be transitions into a utopian world which differ immensely from those depicted by More, Swift, Butler, or Wells. No Wellsian interplanetary traveller could be moved to the following thoughts:

> 'He wondered how he could ever have thought of planets, even of the Earth, as islands of life and reality floating in a deadly void. Now, with a certainty which never after deserted him, he saw the planets—the "earths" he called them in his thought—as mere holes or gaps in the living heaven—excluded and rejected wastes of heavy matter and murky air, formed not by addition to, but by subtraction from, the surrounding brightness. And yet, he thought, beyond the solar system the brightness ends. Is that the

real void, the real death? Unless . . . he grasped for the idea . . . unless visible light is also a hole or gap, a mere diminution of something else. Something that is to bright unchanging heaven as heaven is to the dark, heavy earth.'[205]

This is hardly a scientific consideration of the nature of space. The journey ceases to be a purely physical one and becomes symbolical. Of course all journeys to utopia have a deeper meaning, because the utopian state somehow or other points to a moral, and because the journey to another world is a transition from the real to the imaginary and ideal. But generally the feeling for this transition is hardly expressed at all. The traditional utopian journey is not an adventure into the unknown with some dimly perceived end luring the traveller onwards. It does not evoke spiritual longing, and is not a quest. More's Hythloday, Bacon's captain, Gulliver, and most of the others are curious travellers, discovering the unknown countries by accident; they are not seekers for the light, although they may be spiritually changed *post factum*. With the emergence of planetary and time journeys it would seem more appropriate for the traveller to be moved by other feelings, but here again the scientific adventurous explorer predominates. Yet the possibility of a deeper spiritual significance inherent in all journeys to utopia has partly been used very early, e.g. in Andreae's *Christianopolis* (1619). But in English literature the utopian account and the allegorical pilgrim's progress remained separate for a long time, and only recently there has been some change. Certain possibilities are foreshadowed in *Erewhon*. There is a deepening of tone which was quite unknown to earlier utopian writers. This applies only to the introductory chapters. Higgs, one of the most inconsistent utopian travellers, is partly a commercial explorer, partly a seeker moved by a sense of mystery and spiritual longing. At certain moments Higgs is the lost wanderer, disturbed by a kind of nostalgia for the unknown country beyond the range, the land of heart's desire.

'Oh, wonderful! wonderful! so lonely and so solemn, with the sad grey clouds above, and no sound save a lost lamb bleating upon the mountain side, as though its little heart were breaking. Then there comes some lean and withered old ewe, with deep, gruff voice and unlovely aspect, trotting back from the seductive pasture; now she examines this gully, and now that, and now she stands listening with uplifted head, that she may hear the distant wailing and obey it. Aha! they see and rush towards each other. Alas! they are both mistaken; the ewe is not the lamb's ewe,

> they are neither kin nor kind to each other, and part in coldness. Each must cry louder, and wander farther yet; may luck be with them both that they may find their own at nightfall.'[206]

Later there is the mysterious portent of Chowbok's strange and frightening ecstasy, then the dream on the mountains, and finally, on the summit of the pass, the awe-inspiring majestic statues, of whose voices Butler said:

> 'One feels them in the diaphragm—they are, as it were, the groaning and labouring of all creation travailing together until now.'[207]

All this might be the opening to an impressive symbolical journey of a soul searching for a spiritual reality, but once in Erewhon, every trace of such beginnings disappears and the playful and critical intellect reigns supreme. Yet a definite step towards a different type of utopian journey has been taken. This possibility of a spiritual utopia has been exploited in W. H. Hudson's *A Crystal Age*. The whole narrative is a quest for the mystery of existence, culminating in the hero's death. The book is pervaded by a dreamlike romantic feeling of an over-soul.

> 'I waited for the last wavelet to fade away, but when the surface was once more still and smooth as dark glass, I began to be affected by the profound silence and melancholy of nature, and by something proceeding from nature—phantom, emanation, essence, I know not what. My soul, not my sense perceived it, standing with finger on lips, there, close; its feet resting on the motionless water which gave no reflection of its image, the clear amber sunlight passing undimmed through its substance.'[208]

But in spite of the concern with the hero's spiritual life and development *A Crystal Age* is not an allegorical journey like *The Pilgrim's Progress*, but a utopia dealing with social questions as well, although the effect created is no longer one of practicability or hard concreteness.

This tendency to blur the clear outlines of the 'classical' utopias is a characteristic of many modern products, and romantic lyrical notes appear in works where the scientific attitude would seem to leave no room for them, e.g. in Charlotte Haldane's *Man's World*. No longer are all the utopias clearly defined regions, however fantastically they may be located in space and time. Many new utopian fantasies seem curiously liquid, their setting one of misty vagueness which finds its appropriate expression in the atmospheric conditions. As in the passage quoted from *Erewhon*, evening, the approach of night, provides the proper emotional background. Such a setting may be highly suggestive, as in the introductory chapters to John Palmer's *The Hesperides*. The theme is similar to that of *The Time Machine* and the exact detail is by no means neglected, but the mood is entirely different. The fading light and the appearance of the stars seem to impart a sense of mystery to every observation and occurrence. There is no longer any attempt to overcome the reader's incredulity by a frontal attack of clever forceful pseudo-scientific argumentation. In such cases the reader is subtly introduced to a sense of wonder, to a condition in which another reality can be accepted with the symbolical change from day to night. The critical intellect is not confused and juggled with; it is gently lulled asleep. In C. S. Lewis's *Out of the Silent Planet* or Herbert Read's *Green Child* the traveller feels lost in the evening gloom, haunted by strange forebodings lurking in the uncertain light. Read's Olivero has great difficulty in ascertaining whether the familiar brook actually runs in a new direction. In spite of the apparently clear narrative something subtly magical has crept into utopian writing.

In some cases it is not even a question of dissolving and surmounting the realistic setting in time and space by skilful handling of the atmosphere. The narrative may have a dreamy vagueness from the very outset, which is the exact opposite of the traditional utopian technique. Such books depict 'landscapes of the soul' and remind the reader of *The Pilgrim's Progress*. As in *Erewhon* there may be a country bordered by a huge mountain-range. Nobody knows what is on the other side.

> 'Living so near the range, I soon accepted it as an essential part of my life, and at one time it represented for me the equivalent of Christian's journey in the Pilgrim's Progress.'[209]

Or there may be 'the border' beyond which there is another mysterious country, as in Rex Warner's *The Wild Goose Chase*. The strange facts are simply accepted. There is no explanation provided for these impossible premises.

Such modern allegorical utopias depart from the realistic method in other ways too. In the *Pilgrim's Progress* we are quite plainly and unmistakably told at the very beginning that it all is a dream. Otherwise the narrative is quite precise and logical. But some modern utopias are not only dreamlike in a certain vagueness of setting, but even where the details are quite clear, the total effect seems curiously distorted. They are 'queer'. At first glance the situation may appear to be vaguely familiar and ordinary; but then some facts intervene which somehow do not quite seem to fit, and these force the reader to penetrate to another level.

> 'All my youth had been haunted by the mountain range that rose suddenly in rocky steps to the west of my home. My old nurse was the widow of a famous guide who had been killed during the first attack on the summit; for it was a peculiarity of the range that the only way to cross it was to climb to the top of the Pale Peak.'[210]

Of course, it may be barely possible that a mountain range only can be crossed by climbing to the highest peak in it, but it is strange enough to make the reader look for another explanation. In time this becomes more and more necessary, since the range cannot even be crossed by aeroplane and the aviator who reaches the top goes mad. Such journeys are far more fantastic than interplanetary travelling, although the most ordinary means of locomotion may be employed.

> 'It seems, though it was many years ago, only yesterday that we citizens of a seaside town, standing in ranks along the esplanade, watched, cheering at the same time with all the force of our lungs the outset of the three brothers who, with the inconsiderate fine daring of youth, were prepared, each in his own way, to go far on bicycles, distinguishing our town by an attempt which even the brothers only dimly understood and which seemed to most of us who stood spectators vociferously cheering impracticable, to some even ridiculous. Young and vigorous they looked, different one from the other, as they wheeled into the square their diverse coloured bicycles, made by the same maker at different dates, and they seemed, by the expression of their faces, already in thought upon the moorland road which was to lead them to the frontier many miles away, where very few of us had ever been, and those few shook their heads with a hint of dangers to be met saying nothing but doubting much, as the rest of us doubted, whether the brothers ever were destined to achieve their purpose, which they all, though very indistinctly, had in view.'[211]

Everything in this description is physically possible, yet the total effect is utterly fantastic. The brothers' aim is 'to go far on bicycles' and the journey seems to be dangerous, but they have neither provisions nor arms. All seem to be agreed that they are going to 'distinguish their town', although nobody knows what it all is about. The accurate information about the colour of the bicycles and the different dates of construction makes everything even stranger. To the sober view the world portrayed in this passage is crazy and by no stretching of the imagination will it ever become realistic. Only a reading at a different level, an allegorical reading, will bring out its essential consistency and coherence, while in fantastic realism a journey to the moon or a planet is self-sufficient. But in spite of that such stories may be enjoyed purely as accounts of fantastic adventures, and sometimes the allegory is by no means obtrusive and reveals itself only gradually without ever assuming the direct distinctness of the *Pilgrim's Progress*. In Herbert Read's *The Green Child* the stream whose direction has been reversed introduces us to the world of fantasy. This reversion may be accepted as a plainly fantastic statement, but a more careful reading shows the underlying symbolism. The traveller Olivero returns from active life to peace at home.

> 'To escape from the sense of time, to live in the eternity of what he was accustomed to call the divine essence of things.'[212]

He arrives at his birth-place, in the evening.

> 'It was then that he noticed, or thought he noticed, an extraordinary fact. The stream as he remembered it . . . ran in the direction of the station from which he had just come. But now, indubitably, it was flowing in the opposite direction, towards the church.'[213]

The approach of night and the stream symbolize Olivero's situation; the return to the timeless divine essence. The stream took its origin there (beyond the church) and it used to flow toward the station out into the world of active life when Olivero was a boy. Now it returns to the source. The third part of the book presents this spiritual utopia after the social utopia of the middle part. It is symbolically situated in the interior of the earth since its concern is with the inner life and also with timelessness. In that subterranean world there is no change of day and night or the seasons; there are no fluctuations whatever. Time has hardly any meaning there. The full symbolism only makes itself felt towards the end. As in most of these utopias the increase of the fantastic element is gradual.

When considering influences on modern utopian writing Kafka's name ought not to be omitted. Warner's and Todd's utopian journeys[214], for instance, are more muscular versions of Kafka's strangely grotesque and dark allegories. These queerly logical nightmares resemble *The Castle* or *The Trial* not only in their narrative technique, but also in the type of hero and his experience. There is a strange elusive authority at work behind all the happenings and the partly passive, partly rebellious hero has the sense of being hunted and played with. Just as the lyrical romantic note creeps into the predominantly scientific utopia, so allegorical symbolism can be found in a type of forecast like *1984*, which on the whole derives its strength from an entirely different, much more factual and realistic presentation. But from time to time the hard matter-of-fact surface cracks and mysterious forces are seen at work, giving the theme a deeper significance by removing it from the purely political level. Especially two elements are to be noted: Winston Smith's unreasoned conviction that he and O'Brien will meet 'where there is no darkness', and the episodes concerned with what may be called the theme song:

> 'It was the lonely hour of fifteen. . . . And then, for perhaps half a minute in all, something happened to the telescreens. The tune that they were playing changed, and the tone of the music changed too. There came into it—but it was something hard to describe. It was a peculiar, cracked, braying, jeering note: in his mind Winston called it a yellow note. And then a voice from the telescreen was singing:
>
> Under the spreading chestnut tree
> I sold you and you sold me:
> There lie they, and here lie we,
> Under the spreading chestnut tree.'[215]

The men hearing the song weep. We do not know why, but later on, after Winston has betrayed Julia, the same thing happens again, and again there is a curious air of unreality about it, quite different from the Two Minutes Hate or similar events:

> 'perhaps it was not happening, perhaps it was only a memory taking on the semblance of sound.'[216]

It is the symbolical summing-up of the ultimate betrayal, when all affectionate ties have been severed and replaced by the principle of mutual distrust, fear, and hate, in an organization which is based on the motto: *homo homini lupus.*

While being strongly allegorical, novels like Herbert Read's *Green Child*, Rex Warner's *Wild Goose Chase*, C. S. Lewis's *Out of the Silent Planet*, or Ruthven Todd's *Over the Mountain* still qualify as utopian. In each of them there are clearly defined imaginary countries with strange institutions separated from ordinary life by barriers of space and time. Moreover the social problems are sufficiently stressed, although man is not reduced to a merely political being. Kafka's *The Castle* on the other hand could hardly be called utopian, and the same holds good for novels like Rex Warner's *The Aerodrome* or *The Professor*. In such books the unrealistic vagueness of the geographical setting and the social problems are only the receding background for the predominantly psychological conflict of the strongly individual hero who is distinct from the functional type of the utopian traveller. But in some cases it may not be quite clear whether an individual psychological problem or a general social one predominates.

In all the works considered the original nature of the utopian technique has been considerably changed. This is partly due to the fact that most of these utopias are allegorical as well as socially constructive; but this change also reflects the general development of utopian fiction: the utopian account slowly assumes the shape of a novel.

4

TOWARDS THE NOVEL

REALISTIC and symbolical utopian journeys are both distinct from the plainly fantastic ones. In the last the extraordinary translation into utopia is just an obvious means to an end, leaving not a moment's doubt about the impossibility of the account. These fantasies are amusingly incredible, without any symbolical meaning shaping the nature of the fantastic distortion. Here we are in the realm of sheer magic, the world of the Arabian Nights. On the whole this type of journey is far less frequent than the realistic or symbolical one. The nature of the journey and the nature of utopia generally correspond, sometimes very intimately, sometimes less so. But a complete divorce can hardly be imagined. A hard, 'practical' utopia and a magical introduction do not seem to agree very well, for the persuasiveness of the utopian society will be imperilled by admitting an element of plain magic. One of the few magical journeys to a constructive utopia can be found in Robert Blatchford's *The Sorcery Shop*. Here a wizard transports two London clubmen to a socialist utopia on the lines of *News from Nowhere*. 'If the introduction is sheer fantasy, why not the rest?' the sceptical reader may ask. Possibly a puzzling pseudo-scientific introduction might force him to admit that reality is not quite as plain as a pikestaff: thus it might prepare him to take a more tolerant attitude to the proposed utopian scheme.

Magical journeys are much more appropriate and effective when, as in Eimar O'Duffy's Irish utopian fantasies, the imaginary country itself does not make any pretence to reality whatever. This reduction of utopian reality can be taken one stage further when it is admitted in the utopian romance itself that the utopian dream is not more than a dream. The attempt to span the gap between the real and the ideal by a bridge of factual details has been given up, and the utopian writer is contented with calling himself a utopian, a dreamer. Such is the case in Morris's *News from Nowhere*. Not even the title is disguised any longer. Practically all the earlier utopian writers showed great versatility in inventing ever new titles for disguising the fact that they are talking of Nowhere. Titles like the original *Utopia*, or *Erewhon*, and many others are the exact equivalent of the realistic journey to utopia. At a first glance they seem to be real place names, but when analysed they reveal their purely imaginary nature. Towards the end of the nineteenth century the change in the utopian's attitude becomes manifest in the titles and subtitles. Before then utopias were called 'descriptions, accounts, discoveries, reports, annals, voyages, records, memoirs,' all pointing to their actuality and all of them employing an ironical approach. Morris and some of the moderns are no longer ironical. A new utopian high seriousness makes itself felt. On the one hand the utopian writer wants to make his imaginary world as concrete as possible; on the other hand, the more serious, practical, and realistic his approach to active political life is, the less he will be ready to indulge in pseudo-serious and pseudo-scientific realism in fiction. So it is only in modern times, when utopianism does not seem so wildly fantastic any longer (at least as regards the material means), that a clear distinction is being made between social reform and utopian romance. It is furthermore a sign that the utopian genre has been definitely established and can be labelled accordingly. Morris calls *News from Nowhere* 'some chapters from a utopian romance.' Blatchford points to the unreality of his work in the title, *The Sorcery Shop*, as well as in the subtitle, 'an impossible romance'. And although the 'descriptions, discoveries, records' continue there is an increasing number of such designations as 'romance, story, tale, dream, vision, prophecy, forecast, myth, fantasy'.

In many of these stories the dream or trance or fever vision forms an important element of the story itself.[217] The journey to utopia is treated as a purely psychological, though specially vivid experience. The hero experiencing it becomes a clinical case.

> 'He was ill for several months, and when he recovered he found himself in considerable doubt as to whether what he remembered had really occurred. It looked very much like a delusion produced by his illness, and most of his apparent adventures could, he saw, be explained psycho-analytically.'[218]

In J. D. Beresford's *What Dreams May Come* (1942) the 'traveller' is gradually conditioned by his early unhappy life to make a neurotic escape into a utopian dream world. The hero's development is minutely analysed from his first faint dream to his final psycho-somatic transformation and breakdown. The portrayal of utopia recedes in the interest of psychological and psycho-analytical observation. In spite of such psychological relativism the utopian vision is accorded some elementary force and reality. It is regarded as an image emerging from something like the collective unconscious.

The final step towards abolishing the illusion of reality is taken when the utopian society is presented in a process of ratiocinative construction, as in Wells's *A Modern Utopia*. There is not even a consistent use any longer of what Wells calls a 'hard' narrative. There is a continual change from conditional speculation to indicative description of utopian institutions which have been derived from such speculations.

> 'I am aiming throughout at a sort of shot-silk texture between philosophical discussion on the one hand and imaginative narrative on the other.'[219]

Treyer[220] traces the decline of utopian writing from Plato onwards to ever more fictional accounts till, in the end, we are left with mere amusing entertainment. Quite apart from the problematical evaluation implied in such a view, it fails to convince with regard to the actual development of the utopian writers' seriousness. In the nineteenth century utopian fiction became more serious, practical, and influential than ever before. Fourier, Cabet, Bellamy, Morris, and Wells in *A Modern Utopia* deal with problems of social reconstruction and planning in a new spirit. In their eyes utopias are less satirical reflections and escapist wish-fulfilments than expectations of practical success. There is more stress on 'how the change came' than before, and *A Modern Utopia* in particular shows the new world in process of construction.

On the one hand abstract philosophical discussions become more important again, but on the other hand the loss of the pseudo-scientific technique of primitive realism makes way for a new approach to the possibilities of utopian fiction. The author is free to point to his utopian world as a deliberate imaginative exercise.

> '*Imagine, if you can,* a small hexagonal shape, like the cell of a bee. It is lighted neither by window nor by lamp, yet it is filled with a soft radiance.'[221]

In other cases this deliberately self-conscious approach to utopia or to the future becomes an element of considerable interest within the frame-work of the story. The imaginative creation of utopia is treated as fiction within fiction, as in John Gloag's *To-Morrow's Yesterday*, where the forecast is presented in the shape of a film. A similar, but more complicated device is used in Aldous Huxley's *Ape and Essence*. Here the future is revealed at two removes from ordinary reality. The world of the future is depicted in a film-script whose technical directions constantly remind the reader of its imaginary character.

> 'Close shot of a characteristic product of progressive technology—a hare-lipped Mongolian idiot. Over the shot we hear the chanting of the chorus.'[222]
> 'The Camera moves from the altar to . . .'
> 'We cut back to the altar.'[223]
> 'We cut to a medium close shot of Dr. Poole.'
> 'Dissolve to the interior of the Unholy of Unholies.'[224]

Moreover the film-script itself is discussed within a contemporary narrative frame. We have moved a long way from the pseudo-scientific naïve or ironical realism which insisted on the greatest possible verisimilitude of the utopian journey. There is no longer any need for a first person narrative to account for the hero's feelings. There are no letters, documents, and other proofs to make the story credible. Fiction has long since been recognized as fiction and, rather late, having established a tradition of its own on which the more recent authors can fall back, utopian fiction follows suit.

Morris passes abruptly into utopia. There is no perceptible journey between the present and the future, but in the end he dissolves the future in a dream. Almost exactly the same technique is employed in Oliver Onions' *The New Moon, a romance of reconstruction* (1918). In the twentieth century the completely frameless utopian novel definitely comes into use. This is not an entirely new departure, but formerly there had only been primitive beginnings like Harrington's *Oceana* (1656), a poorly disguised cabalistic history. On the other hand there were the fairy tale and fable. Some of the modern frameless utopian stories derive from this type, especially when they are satirically fantastic like G. K. Chesterton's *The Flying Inn*, Robert Nichols's *Golgatha & Co.*, C. E. Montague's *Right Off the Map*, or George Orwell's *Animal Farm*. But the more realistic frameless utopian novel is a new development. In the ordinary realistic novel the author does not have to explain how he comes to know about his characters' innermost feelings and thoughts. 'Why should I adopt a different technique?' the modern utopian writer seems to ask himself. 'Is the modern reader not steeped in utopian imagination and thought?' So the author's supposed direct knowledge of utopia is accepted as a matter of course and the imaginary world can be presented straight away without any danger of confusing a reader who has become used to such creations. Sometimes the old way of introducing the reader to utopia is ironically discounted:

> 'It was Dr. Ransom who first saw that our only chance was to publish in the form of fiction what would certainly not be listened to as fact.'[225]

In spite of the strong movement from pseudo-scientific realism towards plain fiction, some authors still feel the need to explain and justify their procedure in prefatory notes. Wells expounds his narrative technique in *A Modern Utopia*, Chesterton enlarges on the use of the prophetic past in his introduction to *The Napoleon of Notting Hill*, and John Collier prefaces his utopian tale *Tom's A-Cold* with a clear programmatic statement about the absence of any pseudo-realistic account:

> 'Having imagined this state of affairs, it has been my business to describe it closely, just as I would a Malayan settlement or a neolithic meal or ceremony, but not to account for it merely because it happens to take place in the future. I believe that, given a certain impetus, things may take this sort of course, and in as short a time, despite the obvious objections, but I am not concerned to document a tale with all the artistic untruths of why and wherefore.'[226]

Many modern writers take all this for granted, and although their descriptive method may be very realistic they plunge straight into the utopian account.[227] This type of utopia is more modern in method than the pseudo-scientific interplanetary or time-journey. After passing through the stages of the 'true' report and subsequent romance, utopia becomes a subject for the novelist. Some writers feel called upon to add an explanatory subtitle, but the best-known and most modern forecasts, *Brave New World*, *1984*, and *Ape and Essence* are simply described as novels. Even Wells's works is affected by this recent development. While his early work had been neatly divided into realistic novels on the one hand, and fantastic and utopian romances on the other, this distinction can no longer be made in the case of *The Holy Terror* (1939).

In most of these books the reader is made acquainted with the utopian world by means of an initial shock of surprise instead of a gradual transition.

'A squat grey building of only thirty-four stories. Over the main entrance the words CENTRAL LONDON HATCHERY AND CONDITIONING CENTRE, and, in a shield, the World State's motto, COMMUNITY, IDENTITY, STABILITY.'[228]

These are the first sentences in *Brave New World*. They come as a shock and at the same time they convey the necessary information and establish the setting. Orwell's introductory paragraph is similar, but subtler in technique.

'It was a bright cold day in April, and the clocks were striking thirteen.'[229]

The next few sentences might occur in any realistic novel. The clocks striking thirteen serve as an introduction to utopia. At a first glance they might simply suggest a crazy world, but even more so a world where life has been rationalized. At the same time the number thirteen is meant to convey an ominous note. The key sentence comprehends the suggestion of craziness, rationalization, and an undefined threat. The next shock, *Hate Week*, which follows at some distance, further develops the initial impression.

Sometimes the shock may be delayed, as in John Collier's *Tom's A-Cold* where a fairly conventional description of a settlement precedes the unmistakable transition into strangeness:

'Just outside the door of the house a heap of rabbit paunchings lay stinking in the midsummer sun. Some dusty hens picked at this carrion, and among these hens a cock strutted up and down. Now and then he opened his wings and stretched his neck as if to crow, but only a creaking sound came, for his tongue was cut out.'[230]

Obviously the England of the future must have slipped back into a state of barbarism if people have to take such precautions against raids from neighbouring settlements. No pseudo-scientific frame is needed. The writer can devote his whole attention to the action within the utopian state.

The utopian narrative of the imaginary journey is necessarily extremely limited in the possible variations of its plot. First there is the realistic setting, the person of the traveller, the journey to utopia, the first acquaintance with the utopian state, an account of its evolution, a more or less detailed description of its institutions, and finally the return to reality. The danger of this kind of plot consists in its lack of continuity and unity. Generally there is a definite break between the breathless physical excitement of the first and last part on the one hand, and the intellectual experience of the middle part on the other. The abruptness of the transitions can be softened by various means, but the visitor remains a passer-by and the plot in the utopian country remains, as it were, a sub-plot, just one experience, although probably the most important one, among an epic string of other experiences. The precarious continuity lies in the visitor's personality. This superficial unity can be turned into a more significant one by making the visitor an original character whose gradual spiritual development can be traced. Of course, this possibility was noticed very early, but since the authors are primarily interested in the visitors as guinea-pigs destined to swallow the utopian patent pills, the almost invariable result is the production of the same old character with different convictions grafted onto him. Not until fairly recently do we get any definite traces of a genuine psychological and spiritual development.[231] Such works seem to indicate that the utopian journey, if it is to survive on a literary level, will have to assume the form of a spiritual and symbolical quest, or it will have to be subjected to a more sophisticated treatment, as in Aldous Huxley's *Ape and Essence*. Of course this does not mean that such a utopian journey of the old type cannot be made into a highly amusing and even brilliantly satirical story if handled by a writer with a fertile invention, shrewd humour, and a keen eye for the incongruous and ridiculous side of ordinary life, but it will need more than these to make his work a novel.

The completely utopian action does away with these difficulties; instead of being restricted to a string of episodes with the visitor on the one side and the utopians on the other, the writer has room for building up a continuous dramatic action in the same medium. In various degrees this has been done in such works as Chesterton's *Napoleon of Notting Hill*, in Rose Macaulay's *What Not*, in *Brave New World*, in *1984* and others. When employing this new kind of plot, modern utopias come nearest to the traditional novel. All the outward characteristics of a novel are there. But what is the status of this type of fiction? What is the literary value of the utopian novel, the most finished product of the utopian tradition?

5

LITERARY ACHIEVEMENT

THE development towards the novel is part of the logical evolution of the myth-creating utopian imagination, which impatiently proceeds from the general idea to ever greater actualization. The evolutionary outlook serves as a strong theoretical basis for the development of particular social hypotheses. These social hypotheses are again particularized by a detailed description which veils the hypothetical character of the imaginary state. The imaginary journey adds further concretion and actualization by linking utopia to a definite place, moment, and psychological situation. The hypothetical character of the utopian creation has still further receded, though still present by ironical implication. When assuming the form of a unified novel, a utopia drops this ironical pseudo-realism. The outside visitor disappears and no longer constantly reminds us of the unreality of the utopian world by his very presence in it. The interest centres in the utopian characters, who are directly presented. These utopians are not seen as a largely homogeneous mass, they are diversified and individualized and become objects of human interest. Moreover, the disintegration of utopian optimism has set in by this time. Utopia is no longer perfect, it is put in doubt, it is full of the social and moral conflicts which have been considered earlier in this study. Utopia is nearer our own imperfect world. At last the utopian writer's aim has been achieved: utopia has come alive, the reader becomes a citizen of the imaginary world. The claims of hypothesis and reality are reconciled, the utopian's impatient desire for creating a new world has found the ideal short cut to the independent realm of full-grown literary fiction.

But even when successful a utopian novel is generally regarded with suspicion; it is not considered to be a novel in the proper meaning of the word:

> 'Novels are nearly always concerned with life as it is or has been lived, and only very exceptionally (and seldom satisfactorily) with life as it might be.'[232]

'The power of fantasy penetrates into every corner of the universe, but not into the forces that govern it—and novels of this type have an improvised air.'[233]

'There is an elementary distinction to be made between the discussion of problems and ideas, and what we find in the great novelists.'[234]

'Every novel is still-born that is laden with transcendental intentions, be they political, ideological, symbolical, or satirical.'[235]

The main objections to utopias as novels may be summed up as follows:

1. Utopian novels are fantastic.
2. They are concerned with ideas instead of characters.
3. They are tendentious.

When considering the objection that a utopian novel is fantastic, we should distinguish two different aspects of utopian fantasy. A utopia will always be superficially fantastic in its description of the imaginary society, even though this imaginary society may be placed in the near future. This type of fantasy can be accepted just as exotic local colour must be accepted in other novels. But the trouble with utopian fantasy of a merely technical kind is that there must be so much of it. A whole new world has to be created.

> 'I am aware that it is dangerous to fly too far. The story teller who soars out of our earthly geography and history altogether starts with too great an emptiness before him. He has to create everything, to tell you everything from the beginning; it cannot be taken for granted that in his superlunary world the sky is still blue, the grass still green. Such excessive freedom is onerous to him and tiresome to you.'[236]

This is especially true of evolutionary fantasies like Stapledon's, but even in a forecast of the near future like *1984* there has to be a considerable amount of introductory description. But despite this, the world thus created generally still has a certain unreal brittle hardness about it. The aim of the utopian novelist will consist in keeping this kind of description as unobtrusive as possible.

The objections raised against the psychological fantasy of the utopian novel are even more serious. Utopian novels are not true to 'human nature'. Of course, they have to present a different type of human nature; but as long as the difference is consistently and convincingly derived from possible experience, as long as the utopian attitude is not too 'superlunary', this difference should be accepted: human nature is after all not very constant. The failure to create a human interest in a utopian novel is very often the failure of the individual writer rather than the failure of the utopian genre.

Then it is true that a utopia needs must be a novel of ideas. Some of its individual characters need not be representatives of certain ideas, they may represent average human beings; but even if that is the case they are always shown in conflict with an environment which is nothing else than an embodiment of the author's political and social hypotheses. If a novel should not be based on such ideas, utopias like so many other works of fiction cannot be called novels.

Then it is also true that a great number of utopias are tendentious, for examples Morris's *News from Nowhere*, or Bellamy's *Looking Backwards*, or Wells's *A Modern Utopia*, and many others. They all put forward a more or less definite programme of social reconstruction made attractive by the colours of wishful thinking. Opposing programmes are discredited. These utopians are social reformers interested in a special programme. They are politicians setting themselves up as prophets proclaiming: 'Such and such a thing should be done. If it were done, all this would certainly happen.'

On the other hand there are the utopian moral philosophers who are not concerned with definite party programmes, but with the possibilities of human nature. Their choice of a theme may be very similar to that of the utopian politicians, but it is differently stated: 'Such and such a thing might happen. If it did, all this might happen for various reasons.' The politician's utopia is a prophetic assertion, the moral philosopher's utopia a speculative enquiry. The moral judgements implied in such enquiring utopias need not be different from those implied in any other novel. They should not be called tendentious.

To sum up: A limited amount of fantasy and the prevalence of social ideas in a utopian novel cannot be avoided and should be accepted as a distinctive feature of the utopian genre; in fact they form some of the main attractions of this type of story. The aim of the skilful utopian novelist will not consist in abolishing such limitations, but he must try to avoid an excessive amount of description, and he must also guard against his actors becoming mere mouthpieces of his ideas. The task is a difficult one; it is quite obvious that he cannot possibly succeed in the same way as the writer of a realistic novel. He must remain content with an approximation. But the degree of such an approximation decides the quality of the utopian narrative as a novel.

Of all the attempts in the direction towards an English utopian novel, Aldous Huxley's *Brave New World* and George Orwell's *1984* must be considered the most successful examples. Other utopias may offer more valuable social ideas, but they fall short as novels; while some related fantasies may be equally good or better novels, these do not face the utopian's task of presenting a plausible social organization, which is to work in a future world subject to the same natural laws as ours.

Brave New World is not a novel of characters, but this does not really matter in this case since it is the very point the book wants to make that in a future world there will not be any individuals who can be called characters. They are only variations of a pattern. In optimistic utopias the threatening loss of individuality is a disadvantage. In pessimistic forecasts it is turned to an advantage. The only real character appears in the person of the Savage, who is the traditional visitor from the outside world in a new disguise.

The book is based on the central idea, 'that human beings are given free will in order to choose between insanity on the one hand and lunacy on the other'.[237] They have to choose between the scientific civilization of utopia and the primitivism of the past. The evolution and discussion of these two antagonistic attitudes require a good deal of space. These historical accounts and discussions generally defeat utopian story-telling. In Bulwer-Lytton's *The Coming Race* the adventurous journey (four chapters) leads up to the introductory description of the people. Then there follow nine central chapters on customs, doctrines, the state of society, religion and their evolution, while the last twelve chapters are mainly taken up by the love intrigue and the final escape. In *Erewhon* the first six chapters describe the journey, four the first acquaintance, the next seventeen chapters concern the evolution of Erewhonian life, and only two are needed for the escape and return. In Morris's *News from Nowhere* the proportion is different again: there is a very short introductory transition, a long stage of getting acquainted with the surface aspects of the utopian society, a long central discussion, which is followed by a protracted idyllic afterglow and an abrupt, short return to reality. Many other instances might be given, where the story follows more or less the same pattern. The historical account is placed in the central part, when the stranger or the strangers and the utopian wise man or men meet and discuss all the important questions connected with the subject. The arrest in the action generally becomes very obtrusive. But even when handled with greater subtlety, as in Wells's *Men Like Gods*, the historical account still interrupts the action and intrudes into the story as something foreign, although it is a necessary part of the whole. The writer is confronted by the dilemma:

which should be given preference, historical plausibility or interesting action?

Of course, the historical or evolutionary account can be so ingenious and interesting in itself that it does not greatly matter whether it is completely integrated or not.

> 'Erewhon was not an organic whole; Erewhon Revisited may fairly claim to be. Nevertheless, though in literary workmanship I do not doubt that this last-named book is an improvement on the first, I shall be agreeably surprised if I am not told that Erewhon, with all its faults, is the better reading of the two.'[238]

Originality of thought and imagination are as important as the construction of a clever plot, but the integration of two elements will make the utopian story a better novel.

Apart from clumsy construction one particular fault of the historical accounts in all the old utopias, and in most of the modern ones, especially interferes with the action: they only stimulate the intellectual curiosity of the reader. The traveller comes to utopia, is dumbfounded by all the strange things he sees, conceives an overwhelming desire to know, and in due course, when the story has reached the central part, he is told all about the origin of the utopian institutions or of utopian man. The past is hardly ever a dramatic problem in such books.

In Wells's *Time Machine* the search for the utopian past becomes an exciting story when the time traveller descends into the interior of the earth in order to learn the truth about the mysterious existence of the Morlocks. Here the enquiry into the past assumes the shape of a physical adventure, but there is no need to treat this theme in such an allegorical way. There are means of obtaining a dramatic conflict of a subtler psychological kind which is more appropriate to the novel.

There is one important slogan on which most utopias are based: stability. In the face of this maxim knowledge about the past becomes a problem, even a danger; for the past contains not only all those forces and processes which led to utopia, but also all those disruptive tendencies and disintegrating attitudes which prevented utopia from being realized for such a long time. This conflict between the past and the utopian present is dramatized in *Brave New World.* In this utopia, history is abolished as far as possible. 'History is bunk'[239] is one of the most important leading principles in this new world. More than that, 'most historical facts are unpleasant',[240] and knowledge of such unpleasant facts may corrupt young and innocent people. Only the world controllers possess forbidden books and thereby have access to the past. In short, history is conceived as a reservation that may be visited by certain privileged and immune people. This idea finds its symbolical expression in the Indian reservation of Malpais (Badland) in New Mexico, in which the past is preserved in real life. The importance of this symbol is further stressed by the fact that the few chapters on the reservation are placed right in the centre of the book, being not only the key to the problems, but to the dramatic structure of the novel as well.

In the first act of this utopian drama we see the wholly stable scientific society at work. In the second act this smooth picture is cracked in two places. First in the historical flashback given by Mustapha Mond, the World Controller, whose starting point is provided by the assumption that history is bunk, unpleasant, and dangerous. At the beginning of Mond's exposé there is a rift between antagonistic past and present, but then this gap is gradually closed. This is partly done by the account of the satisfactory development leading to the new society, partly by an adequate literary technique. At first, large lumps of the narrated past and the surrounding present are opposed to each other, then, gradually, the sections from the different reels become shorter and shorter until they finally merge into each other in a whirling double exposure where one sphere cannot be distinguished from the other. The past has been absorbed and annihilated by the dominant section of the community, the World Controller and his audience. In official circles stability proceeds. But the theme of conflict is taken up for the second time in an individual case. Bernard Marx is dissatisfied with utopia. His dissatisfaction finally results in a visit to the reservation in New Mexico. Here the third act of the drama is enacted. The rift between past and utopian present is complete; the picture theoretically destroyed by Mustapha Mond is shown to be a living reality for a small number of people in whose minds the utopian present is non-existent. The deepening of the theme and the preparation for a more dramatic conflict leads to a change of protagonists. Bernard Marx, whose feeble dissatisfaction with utopian society served as an introduction to the vital past, becomes a background figure, and the Savage from Malpais occupies the centre of the stage. The fourth act is a dramatized version of the second act: a meeting of past and present: the Savage is introduced to utopia and violently reacts against the uncongenial surroundings, until the final clash cannot be avoided. While in the second act past and present are juxtaposed, not interfering, but finally merging into each other, here they clash in dramatic dialogue between the World Controller and the Savage.

Again the past is defeated, but this time the rift is not closed, for the highly questionable nature of this stabilized society has been laid bare and a sense of loss is conveyed by the final development, the suicide of the Savage.

Huxley's spiral movement from utopian stability to the reservation of the past and back to a questionable stability effectively absorbs the historical account into the novel. What in earlier utopias is no more than material for the shaping of the utopian conditions and for incidental surprise, here becomes the centre of a coherent dramatic action.

All the stuff of utopian description is there, but it is presented with far more artistry. The principles and the dominant mood of utopia are effortlessly summed up on the first page. There is no pseudo-naïve surprise, no laboured enumeration of unknown facts; utopia is taken for granted. The striking facts are introduced incidentally. There is no trace of the slow plodding movement which is a characteristic of former utopias. The love story is not mere added romantic interest, but serves to bring the inner conflict to its most striking and significant conclusion. *Brave New World* is a well-balanced dramatic novel.

Yet in Aldous Huxley's eyes 'its defects as a work of art are considerable.'[241]

> 'For the sake of dramatic effect the Savage is often permitted to speak more rationally than his upbringing among the practitioners of a religion that is half fertility cult and half Penitente ferocity would actually warrant.'[242]

This is certainly a defect in the delineation of the main character of the book. But in Huxley's eyes the main defect of the book is a different one. *Brave New World* should offer a truly constructive possibility, a third community.

> 'In this community economics would be decentralist and Henry-Georgian, politics Kropotkinesque and co-operative.' etc.[243]
> 'Thus altered, *Brave New World* would possess an artistic and (if it is permissible to use so large a word in connection with a work of fiction) a philosophical completeness, which in its present form it evidently lacks.'[244]

Judging on the 'lower' level of mere fiction it is fortunate that this third possibility has not been introduced. Otherwise *Brave New*

World would have become one of those tendentious utopias advocating a definite political programme.

While *Brave New World* is a brilliant intellectual *tour de force*, *1984* is a utopia of personal experience. *Brave New World* can be regarded as a utopian *Point Counter Point*, presenting a mosaic of conflicting attitudes. *1984* should be seen in connection with a novel like *Coming up for Air*, where Orwell's *homme moyen sensuel*, the middle-aged travelling salesman, goes in search for the simple pleasures of his youth, trying to escape from the artificiality and fear of modern civilization. Most of the central themes of *1984* are contained in *Coming up for Air* (1939):

The Two Minutes Hate and Hate Week:

> 'It was a voice that sounded as if it could go on for a fortnight without stopping. . . . The same thing over and over again. Hate, hate, hate. Let's all get together and have a good hate. Over and over again. It gives you the feeling that something has got inside your skull and is hammering down on your brain.'[245]

The Tortures in the Ministry of Love; and the Big Brother Posters:

> 'Smash! Right in the middle! The bones cave in like an eggshell and what was a face a minute ago is just a great big blob of strawberry jam. Smash! There goes another.'[246]
> 'The barbed wire! The slogans! The enormous faces!'[247]

Furthermore there are the constant fear of war, the drab, joyless wife, the squalid town, the distasteful substitute food, the feeling of being watched and followed when escaping into the country. Then the tormenting desire for something different:

> 'Call it peace, if you like, but when I say peace I don't mean absence of war, I mean peace, a feeling in your guts. And it's gone for ever if the rubber truncheon boys get hold of us.'[248]

In *1984* it's gone for ever; all the fears of the earlier novel have become externalized in a utopia which is deeply rooted in the present. There is less technical fantasy than in *Brave New World* and less superficial brilliancy, but the world of *1984* is far more solid, more individualized. The hero is a human being at home in the utopian world, not a primitive *ingénu*. Winston Smith is far more of a character than any of the persons in *Brave New World*. As in *Coming*

Up for Air, the narrative is a kind of interior monologue interrupted by occasional flash-backs.

We are introduced to Winston Smith at the moment when he decides to seek his own way, thereby committing treason. He wants to see things clearly and to formulate them to himself independently. In order to arrive at an individual solution he first has to recapitulate what he knows. The reader's introduction to utopian conditions takes place as he follows the feverish processes in Winston's mind. This introduction is at once individual and general. It is also the starting point for a double dramatic tension. Will Winston be detected? This question provides the first element of suspense. The sense of doom pervading the book from the beginning suggests an affirmative answer to this question. So a second kind of suspense is created: the action takes the form of a race against time. Will he arrive at the meaning of utopia before he is caught and punished?

As in many other utopias the search for the underlying idea of utopia becomes a search for the past. This story of Winston's adventure with the past is enacted in three parts. The first part begins with his criminal decision to keep a diary. He takes stock of the political and of his personal situation by exploring his own past. We see him living through the daily utopian routine with his consciousness heightened by his search and his fear of detection. It is not only the reader, but also the hero himself who experiences utopia, as it were, for the first time and quite possibly for the last time as well. While looking for fellowship Winston regards different types of utopian citizens with newly gained penetration. In his various attempts at exploration he always ends up against a blank wall.

'I understand HOW: I do not understand WHY.'[249]

However there seems to be some hope in the person of O'Brien.

The second part contains the climax and catastrophe. Winston meets Julia, another individual rebelling against the state. Their love story is the consummation of their desire for the peace of past times. It also exposes all the incredible restrictions by which private life is hemmed in on every side. Their meeting with O'Brien, their oath and drinking to the past is the last decisive criminal act. When having reached the highest point of his anti-utopian *hubris*, while lying peacefully in bed with Julia, in an old-fashioned room in the proletarian quarter, and while perusing the secret key to utopian philosophy, nemesis steps in. Winston and Julia are arrested by the thought-police, just as Winston is on the point of discovering the WHY.

The third part brings the nightmarish revelation. In the torture chambers of the Ministry of Love O'Brien, who turns out to be a member of the thought police, expounds the underlying principle of the Oceanian state: power for power's sake. Inflicting pain and suffering heightens the consciousness of power. Therefore the more pain there is the more powerful and godlike is the privileged class inflicting such pains. By the application of modern science Winston's resistance is completely broken. He accepts the present, which contains the past as well as the future. As O'Brien sums up: there was learning, there was understanding, there was acceptance. Winston's tragedy is the triumph of the Party, which will go on for ever.

1984 is a well-constructed utopian novel, but above all it impresses by the sheer force of imaginative personal experience. But all this does not dispel the impression that there is still a good deal of undigested material, that there is too much political and social theory. As with most utopias one still has the feeling that a second book in the same utopian world would be more successful as a novel. So many things could be left unsaid, so much might be merely implied, and then there could be far more of that differentiation which is necessary for a realistic psychological novel.

1984 is a utopian 'De Profundis'. The genuineness of its despairing mood cannot be doubted, but just because of this it is artistically less satisfactory than *Brave New World*. A utopia cannot bear such tragedy. A utopian tragedy tends to be hysterical or sentimental. Being seriously crushed by a utopian hypothesis is the sign of a morbidly brooding mind. Too much feeling is spent on an inappropriate object. Utopian realism creates only pseudo-reality, the fictitiousness of which must remain quite obvious. If the utopian author wants to escape emotional sensationalism, he should restrain his seriousness and not step beyond the limits of utopian tragi-comedy.

In the course of this study a great many characteristic features of the utopian novel have been considered. Their logical evolution has been traced and the various features have been shown to be parts of an imaginative whole, which may be described as the outcome of the utopian's original desire to create an earthly paradise. But, quite apart from the imaginative details, this attempt must carry with it its own distinctive mood. This utopian mood should be carefully distinguished from the various emotions aroused by certain definite utopian possibilities. It is comprehensive and equally tinctures utopian joy and fear. The presence or absence of this mood decides whether a utopian is in touch with the living reality from which only a work of art can rise, or whether he is just a fantast, skimming the surface. This mood is akin to utopian irony: it is tragicomic. Irony expresses the utopian's double consciousness on an intellectual level, and it is mainly concerned with the utopian fiction, the semblance of facts. Utopian tragicomedy also expresses a double consciousness, intellectual insight is part of it, but it also goes deeper and touches the heart; it lays bare the very root of the utopian idea and is the utopian's final response to that idea.

It is significant that irony becomes less important as the utopian novel gradually frees itself from the fetters of scientific realism, whereas utopian tragicomedy persists. A strong comic element is present in most utopias. The very existence of a utopia is a 'châtiment de la raideur' par excellence. Utopia falls out of place and causes surprised amusement, and therefore a utopian narrative can hardly help being a comedy of situation. But it is also the comedy of manners, ridiculing contemporary society by utopian contrast. But a utopian should not over-emphasize the comic aspect. If he does his creation appears merely irresponsible. A genuine utopia is never purely comic; for it is the creation of a humanist idealist, who seriously desires the happiness of mankind. But the great utopians do not confound the ideal with reality. For them the ideal and the real remain irreconcilable. So there are no happy endings in the greater utopias, but there cannot be any despair either, because the ideal remains inviolate.

> 'There is a common notion that the reading of a Utopia should end with a swelling heart and clear resolves, with lists of names, formation of committees, and even the commencement of subscriptions. But this utopia began upon a philosophy of fragmentation and ends, confusedly, amidst a gross tumult of immediate realities, in dust and doubts, with, at the best, one individual's aspiration.'[250]

In the earlier utopias similar convictions are expressed towards the end.

> ' "You speak of the city whose foundation we have been describing, which has its being in words; for there is no spot on earth, I imagine, where it exists."
> "No", I said; "but perhaps it is laid up in heaven as a pattern for him who wills to see, and seeing, to found a city in himself. Whether it exists anywhere or ever will exist, is no matter".'[251]

> 'So must I nedes confesse and graunt that many thinges be in

> the Utopian weale publique, whiche in our cities I maye rather wishe for, then hope after.'[252]

The modern utopians are even more sceptical. The utopian 'grasps at the Universe and attains—Bathos.'[253]

The minor, naïve utopian, who is not aware of this gap, seriously thinks that he can realize his ideal. Comedy and tragedy are no great concern of his. Above all he wants to be 'practical', but in artistry he only attains bathos. The major, experienced utopian knows that he lives in two separate worlds. His is a double vision. When he is detachedly looking down at reality from the superhuman utopian level, humanity's shortcomings are comic; when longingly looking up to the ideal from the world of human misery, the failure of humanity to rise to the utopian level strikes him as tragic. Unlike the minor utopian he does not seriously think that he can realize his ideal but just because of this he escapes literary bathos. His ambivalent attitude can find perfect expression in the hybrid medium of utopian tragicomedy. In More's *Utopia* this laughter mixed with sadness arises only occasionally because the contrasting action is very limited. But from *Gulliver's Travels* onwards, when the ideal and the real are more continuously interwoven by the contrasting narrative, tragicomedy becomes a distinctive feature of all the most sincerely imaginative utopian novels. Occasionally utopian laughter may be mixed with bitterness rather than sadness, and tragicomedy is reduced to satire; but though a true utopia may be as bitter as *Gulliver's Travels* it will always transcend mere satire and social criticism. It also transcends the monistic myth of godlike man and becomes a valid symbolical formula for the irresolvable paradox of human dualism.

This is the true function of utopia, which is implied in the very word 'utopia'. It designates non-existence and existence at the same time. It reveals the awareness that the ideal does not exist in the world of things. But this negation is hidden. On the surface the word strikingly asserts the living presence of the ideal. Yet the hidden negation reduces its substance. The ideal is alive and present, but only in a world of imagination. This restriction was soon lost sight of:

> 'Wherefore not Utopie, but rather rightely
> My name is Eutopie.'[254]

Eutopia does not contain any hidden negation. It becomes an inspiring belief, a principle of action. The foundations for an earthly paradise seem to be laid. The forecasts constructed on this basis jar upon the reader's mind because of their facile optimism. The more intelligent twentieth-century speculations demonstrate that such a belief is somewhat ill-founded. The former interpretation is reversed: 'Wherefore not Eutopie, but rather rightely my name is Utopie.' But now it is Utopia with a difference. By measuring Utopia against Eutopia, the formerly hidden negation becomes painfully obvious, while the ideal is only present as an implied mental contrast. All the same a sane sceptical balance between the ideal and the real has again been achieved.

Thus the failure of eutopian optimism does not spell the end of a long tradition, but becomes the living source of modern utopian fiction.

NOTES

INTRODUCTION, *pages* xi–xii

[1] e.g. von Mohl (1855); Kaufmann (1879); Kleinwächter (1891); von Kirchenstein (1892); various English and American authors later on, cp. Bibliography.

[2] Hertzler, J. O. (1922); Mumford, Lewis (1923); Mannheim, Karl (1936), cp. Bibliography.

[3] Dupont, V.: *L'Utopie et le Roman Utopique dans la Littérature Anglaise*, Paris 1941.

PART ONE, 1, *pages* 3–14

[4] More: *Utopia*, Ralph Robinson's translation 1551, Dent & Sons, London 1910, p. 119.

[5] Patch, H. R.: *The Other World, according to descriptions in Medieval Literature*, Cambridge, Mass. 1950; Nutt, A., in *The Voyage of Bran, Son of Febal, to the Land of the Living*, ed. by Meyer, K., London 1895; Hastings *Encyclopedia of Religion and Ethics* ('Abode of the Blessed').

[6] *The Travels of Sir John Mandeville*, London 1900, p. 180, and also the greater part of the 33rd chapter.

[7] Quoted in Sir Walter Raleigh's *The English Voyages of the Sixteenth Century*, Glasgow 1906, p. 17.

[8] Huizinga, J.: *Homo Ludens, a Study of the Play Element in Culture*, London 1949, p. 129.

[9] Vaihinger, H.: *The Philosophy of As If, a System of the Theoretical, Practical, and Religious Fictions of Mankind*, London 1929, p. 12.

[10] Sidney, Sir Philip: *An Apology for Poetry, English Critical Essays, 16th, 17th and 18th Centuries*, ed. by E. D. Jones, Oxford 1922, p. 16.

[11] The best account of the Greek utopian novel is to be found in Rohde, E.: *Der Griechische Roman und seine Vorläufer*, Leipzig 1900.

[12] Treyer, Hans: *Die Politische Insel*, Leipzig 1936, p. 82.

[13] A description by the fifth-century writer Dracontius, quoted by H. R. Patch, op. cit., p. 139.

[14] see Note 5.

[15] *Utopia*, p. 73.

[16] *Utopia*, p. 72.

[17] Bacon, Francis: *New Atlantis*, Works, ed. by Basil Montagu, 16 vols., London 1825, vol. II, p. 348.

[18] *New Atlantis*, p. 348.

[19] *New Atlantis*, p. 361.

[20] *New Atlantis*, p. 363.

[21] *New Atlantis*, p. 364–5.

[22] Bacon's exact words are: 'three thousand years ago, *or somewhat more*', which may be a cautious way of evading biblical authority, p. 341.

[23] Huxley, J. S.: *Evolution and Ethics*, London 1947, p. 133.

[24] Huxley, J. S.: *The Uniqueness of Man*, London 1941, p. 287.

[25] Huxley, J. S.: *Evolution, the Modern Synthesis*, London 1942, p. 576.

[26] Huxley, J. S.: *The Uniqueness of Man*, p. 266–7 (in essay on 'Scientific Humanism').

[27] Huxley, J. S.: *Man in the Modern World*, London 1947, p. 146.

[28] Wells, H. G.: *A Modern Utopia*, Chapter 1, § 1.

[29] Treyer, H., op cit., p. 32.

[30] Wells, H. G.: *The Shape of Things To Come, the Ultimate Revolution*, London 1933, p. 432.

[31] Reade, W.: *The Martyrdom of Man* (1872), reprint, London 1934, p. 413.

[32] *The Martyrdom of Man*, p. 437.

[33] Huxley, J. S.: *The Uniqueness of Man*, p. 276.

[34] Huxley, J. S.: *Evolution*, p. 571.

[35] Huxley, J. S.: *The Uniqueness of Man*, p. 274.

[36] Wells, H. G.: *The Shape of Things to Come*, p. 431.

[37] Huxley, J. S.: *Evolution and Ethics*, p. 193–4.

[38] Wells, H. G.: *The Anatomy of Frustration, a modern synthesis*, London 1936, p. 7.

[39] Jaspers, Karl: *Man in the Modern Age* (Die Geistige Situation der Gegenwart), London 1932, p. 235.

PART ONE, 2, *pages* 15–26

[40] Stapledon, *Last and First Men, a Story of the Near and Far Future*, London 1930, p. v–vi.

[41] Haldane, J. B. S.: *Possible Worlds*, London 1927, p. 310–11.

[42] Shaw, G. B.: *Back to Methuselah*, Works, London 1930, vol. 16, p. lxxxix.

[43] *Back to Methuselah*, p. lxxxix–xc.

[44] Stapledon: *Last and First Men*, p. vi.

[45] *Last and First Men*, p. vi.

[46] *Last and First Men*, p. v.

[47] Wells, H. G.: *A Modern Utopia*, Chapter I, § 6.

[48] *Modern Utopia*, Chapter 8, § 1.

[49] Wells, H. G.: *Men Like Gods*, London 1923, p. 24.

[50] *Men Like Gods*, p. 25.

[51] Bulwer-Lytton, E.: *The Coming Race* (1871), Routledge, London 1886, p. 127.

[52] *The Coming Race*, p. 22.

[53] *The Coming Race*, p. 41.

[54] Stapledon, O.: *Last and First Men* (1930); O'Neill, Joseph: *The Land Under England* (1935); Meredith, Edgar: *Our Stranger, a Kinemato-Romance* (1936); Beresford, J. D.: *What Dreams May Come* (1941), etc.

[55] Ollivant, Alfred: *To-Morrow*, London 1927.

[56] *Utopia*, p. 49.

[57] *Utopia*, p. 53.

[58] *The Coming Race*, p. 64.

[59] *The Coming Race*, p. 143. Here as in *Erewhon* eugenic principles are important. This theme is exploited in a great number of utopias, e.g. Vaughan, H. M.: *Meleager* (1916); Macaulay, Rose: *What Not* (1918); Haldane, Charlotte: *Man's World* (1926); Grierson, F. D.: *Heart of the Moon* (1928); Tillyard, Aelfrida: *Concrete* (1930); Wright, S. F.: *The New Gods Lead* (1932), etc.

[60] *The Coming Race*, p. 147.

[61] Chesterton, G. K.: *The Napoleon of Notting Hill*, London 1904, p. 14.

[62] *The Napoleon of Notting Hill*, p. 15.

[63] Meredith, E.: *Our Stranger*, London 1936.

[64] Beresford, J. D. and Wynne-Tyson, Esmé: *The Riddle of the Tower*, London 1944.

[65] Stapledon, O.: *Last and First Men*, p. 198.

[66] *Last and First Men*, p. 306.

PART ONE, 3, *pages* 27–44

[67] see p. 11.

[68] Huxley, Aldous: *Perennial Philosophy*, London 1947.

[69] Bacon: *New Atlantis*, p. 365 and 367.

[70] The fantasies concerned with this theme are very numerous, e.g. Lewis, R. M.: *The Divine Gift* (1906); Barlow, J. W.: *The Immortals' Great Quest* (1909); Gubbins, H.: *The Elixir of Life, or, 2905* A.D. (1914); Wells, H. G.: *Men Like Gods* (1923); Ollivant, A.: *To-Morrow* (1927); Hilton, James: *Lost Horizon* (1933); Shiel, M. P.: *The Young Men Are Coming* (1937); Nott, K.: *The Dry Deluge* (1947).

[71] Other satires of this kind: Gloag, John: *Winter's Youth* (1934); Parkinson, H. F.: *They Shall Not Die* (1939). In this last book one third of the population becomes immortal, but when these immortals reach the age of 150 their souls leave the surviving bodies in a maniacal fit.

[72] Haldane, J. B. S.: *Possible Worlds*, p. 287.

[73] Wells, H. G.: *Men Like Gods*, p. 280.

[74] Wells, H. G.: *The Time Machine*, Dent & Sons, London 1935, p. 295.

[75] e.g. Hodgson, W. H.: *The Night Land* (1912); Guest, Ernest: *At the End of the World, a Vision* (1929).

[76] Stapledon: *Last and First Men*, p. 343.

[77] Wells, H. G.: *Modern Utopia*, Chapter 9, § 7.

[78] ibidem.

[79] in Haldane, J. B. S.: *Possible Worlds*.

[80] *Possible Worlds*, p. 302.

[81] Lewis, C. S.: *Out of the Silent Planet*, London 1938, p. 199–200.

[82] *Out of the Silent Planet*, p. 223.

[83] Haldane: *Possible Worlds*, p. 301.

[84] Orwell, George: *1984*, London 1949, reset ed. 1950, p. 271.

[85] *1984*, p. 271.

[86] *1984*, p. 275.

[87] *1984*, p. 275.

[88] *1984*, p. 275.

[89] Wells, H. G.: *Mind at the End of its Tether*, London 1945, p. 19.

[90] Wells, H. G.: *War of the Worlds*, London 1898, p. 110.

[91] *War of the Worlds*, p. 132.

[92] Cantril, Hadley: *The Invasion from Mars, a Study in the Psychology of Panic, with the complete script of the famous Orson Welles Broadcast*, Princeton 1940.

[93] Cantril: *Invasion from Mars*, p. 52. There are other utopian fantasies in which man is superseded by intelligent animals, e.g. Ridley, F. H.: *The Green Machine* (1926); Gloag, John: *To-Morrow's Yesterday* (1932).

[94] e.g. Beresford, J. D.: *A Common Enemy* (1942); Wells, H. G.: *In the Days of the Comet* (1906).

[95] Lewis, C. S.: *Out of the Silent Planet*, p. 49–50.

[96] Flecker, J. E.: *The Last Generation, a Story of the Future*, London 1922, p. 11 (originally published in 1908). A similar theme is treated in Kernahan, Coulson: *A World Without a Child* (1905).

[97] Lewis, C. S.: *Out of the Silent Planet*, p. 222.

[98] Wells, H. G.: *War of the Worlds*, p. 161.

[99] Wells, H. G.: *Men Like Gods*, p. 282.

[100] Flecker, J. E.: *The Last Generation*, p. 32.

[101] Knox, Ronald E.: *Memories of the Future: Being Memoirs of the Years 1915–1972, written in the Year of Grace 1988 by Opal, Lady Porstock*, London 1923, p. 70–1.

PART TWO, 1, *pages* 45–49

[102] Engels, F.: *Socialism, Utopian and Scientific*, London 1892, p. 72.

[103] Blatchford, Robert: *The Sorcery Shop* (1907); Cassius Minor (pseudonym): *The Finding of Mercia* (1909); Ashbee, C. R.: *The Building of Thelema* (1910); Petworth, A.: *The Little Wicket Gate* (1913); Unitas (pseud.): *The Dream City* (1920); Gunpat (pseud.): *Harilek, a Romance of Modern Central Asia* (1923); Wells, H. G.: *Men Like Gods* (1923); Winch, E.: *The Mountain of Gold* (1928); Beresford, J. D.: *What Dreams May Come* (1941); Lister, Stephen: *Hail Bolonia!* (1948).

[104] Huxley, Aldous: *Science, Liberty, and Peace*, London 1947, p. 48.

[105] Orwell, George: *James Burnham and the Managerial Revolution*, London 1946.

[106] Mannheim, Karl: *Man and Society in an Age of Reconstruction*, London 1940, p. 239.

Part Two, 2, *pages* 50–60

[107] *Utopia*, p. 98.

[108] Bacon: *Novum Organon*, works, vol. 9, p. 281.

[109] Bacon: *New Atlantis*, p. 371.

[110] Morris, William: *News from Nowhere*, Works, 24 vols., London 1912, vol. 16, p. 97.

[111] Morris: *News from Nowhere*, p. 162.

[112] Bellamy, Edward: *Looking Backward 2000–1887*, Random House, New York (Modern Library), p. 90.

[113] Warner, Rex: *The Wild Goose Chase*, London 1937, p. 372–3.

[114] Wells: *Modern Utopia*, Chapter 3, § 6. Other modern utopias expressing similarly optimistic beliefs in science are extremely numerous. Only some of them can be mentioned here: Carrell, F.: *2010* (1914); Wells, H. G.: *Men Like Gods* (1923); Haldane, Charlotte: *Man's World* (1926); Ollivant, A.: *To-Morrow* (1927); Meredith, E.: *Our Stranger*: (1936); Viscount Samuel: *An Unknown Island* (1942); Capon, P.: *The Other Side of the Sun* (1950).

[115] Bulwer-Lytton: *The Coming Race*, p. 24.

[116] e.g. in James Hanley's *What Farrar Saw* (1946), England becomes one huge traffic jam which can only be loosened up by the use of bombs.

[117] Wells, H. G.: *The Sleeper Awakes*, p. 46–7.

[118] Aeroplane fantasies are fairly frequent: Wells, H. G.: *The War in the Air* (1908); Kipling, Rudyard: *As Easy as ABC* (1912) (World dominated by *A*erial *B*oard of *C*ontrol); Warner, Rex: *The Aerodrome* (1941); Arlen, Michael: *Man's Mortality* (1933) (World dominated by IAA, *I*nternational *A*ircraft and *A*irways, Inc.); Stuart, Francis: *Glory* (1933) (World dominated by Trans-Continental Aero-Routes), etc.

[119] Low, A. M. (D.Sc.): *Our Wonderful World of To-Morrow, a Scientific Forecast of the Men, Women, and the World of the Future*, London 1934, p. 271.

[120] Low: *Wonderful World*, p. 257.

[121] Huxley, A.: *Brave New World*, coll. works, p. 1.

[122] Todd, Ruthven: *The Lost Traveller*, London 1944, p. 26–7. Some utopian thrillers exclusively treating the theme of the omnipotent scientist: Kuppard, Skelton (pseud.): *A Fortune From the Sky* (1902); Griffith, G.: *The Great Weather Syndicate* (1906); Maclure, V.: *Ultimatum* (1924); Powell, G.: *All Things New* (1926); Newman, B.: *Armoured Doves* (1931), etc., etc.

[123] Andreae, Johann Valentin: *Christianopolis* (1619); Campanella, Tomaso: *Civitas Solis*: (1623); Gott, Samuel: *Nova Solyma* (1648).

[124] Modern religious utopias are rare, e.g. Hett, John: *Our Glorious Future* (1931) (Science and religion reconciled, a very naïve effort); Rowland, James: *While England Slept* (1932) (Miraculous religious rebirth of England).

[125] Tillyard, Aelfrida: *Concrete, a Story of Two Hundred Years Hence* (1930).

[126] Haldane, Charlotte: *Man's World* (1926).

PART TWO, 3, *pages* 61–67

[127] Low, E. M.: *Our Wonderful World of To-Morrow*, p. 272.

[128] Wells, H. G.: *Modern Utopia*, Chapter 7, § 7.

[129] Wells, H. G.: *The Sleeper Awakes*, p. 45.

[130] Warner, Rex: *The Wild Goose Chase*, p. 220.

[131] *The Wild Goose Chase*, p. 231.

[132] e.g. Mumford, L.: *The Culture of Cities* (1938); Town and Country Planning Text Book ed. by APRR (Association for Planning and Regional Reconstruction) London 1950; Geddes, Patrick: *Cities in Evolution*, London 1949, etc.

[133] Anon. *What Might Have Been, the Story of a Social War* (1907); Newte, H. C.: *The Master Beast, being the true account of the ruthless tyranny inflicted on the British people by Socialism* A.D. *1888–2020* (1907); Mayne, J. D.: *The Triumph of Socialism and how it succeeded* (1908); Anon.: *Red England, a Tale of Socialist Terror* (1909); Everett, F.: *John Bull: Socialist* (1909); Le Queux, W.: *The Unknown To-Morrow, How the Rich Fared at the Hands of the Poor together with a full account of the Social Revolution in England* (1910); Prince, E.: *Wake Up, England, being the Amazing Story of John Bull Socialist* (1910).

[134] Bellamy, E.: *Looking Backward*, p. 42.

[135] Wells, H. G.: *Modern Utopia*, Chapter 9, § 2.

[136] e.g. Benson, R. H.: *Lord of the World* (1907); Wells, H. G.: *The Sleeper Awakes* (1910); Kipling, Rudyard: *As Easy as ABC* (1912); Gregory, O.: *Meccania, the Super State* (1918); Macaulay, Rose: *What Not* (1918); Nichols, Robert: *Golgatha & Co.* (1923); Forster, E. M.: *The Machine Stops* (1928); Grierson, F. D.: *Heart of the Moon* (1928); Tillyard, Aelfrida: *Concrete* (1930); Huxley, Aldous: *Brave New World* (1932); O'Neill, Joseph: *The Land Under England* (1935); Palmer, John: *The Hesperides* (1936); Macowan, N.: *Glorious Morning* (1939); Beresford, J. D.: *The Riddle of the Tower* (1944); Colvin, Ian: *Domesday Village* (1948); Guerard, A. J.: *Night Journey* (1951); Huxley, Aldous: *Ape and Essence* (1949).

PART TWO, 4, *pages* 68–77

[137] *Utopia*, p. 80.

[138] *Utopia*, p. 71.

[139] Plato: *Republic*, V, 459, transl. by A. D. Lindsay (Everyman).

[140] for role of education in general cp. Massò, Gildo: *Education in Utopias*, Columbia University Press, 1927.

[141] Bryson, Lyman: *Science and Freedom*, New York 1947, p. 173.

[142] Montague, C. E.: *Right Off the Map* (1927); Gloag, John: *To-Morrow's Yesterday* (1932); Dearmer, G.: *Saint on Holiday* (1933); Green, F. L.: *A Fragment of Glass* (1947).

[143] Moore, F. F.: *The Marriage Lease* (1907); Haldane, Charlotte: *Man's World* (1926); O'Duffy, Eimar: *The Spacious Adventures of the Man in the Street* (1928); Palmer, John: *The Hesperides* (1936); Warner, Rex: *The Wild Goose Chase* (1937); Capon, P.: *The Other Side of the Sun* (1950).

[144] *1984*, p. 130. Other utopias where socialized sex loses its attraction: Tillyard, Aelfrida: *Concrete* (1930); Palmer, John: *The Hesperides* (1936).

[145] *1984*, p. 273.

[146] Utopian fantasies mainly concerned with the equality of the sexes: Anon.: *Star of the Morning, a Chronicle of Karyl the Great and the Revolt of 1920–22* (1906); Reeth, A.: *Legions of the Dawn* (matriarchy); Wilson, J.: *When the Women Reign* (1908); Fox-Davies, A. C.: *The Sex Triumphant* (1909); Minnett, Cora: *The Day After To-Morrow* (1911); Housman, Laurence: *John of Jingalo* (1912); Anon.: *When Woman Rules, a Tale of the First Women's Government* (1923); Cross, V.: *Martha Brown, M.P. a Girl of To-Morrow* (1935); Guesswell, E. K. (pseud.): *When Yvonne Was Dictator* (1935).

[147] *1984*, p. 253.

[148] *1984*, p. 261.

[149] *1984* (The Principles of Newspeak), p. 305.

[150] *1984*, p. 318.

[151] *1984*, p. 262.

[152] In a recent Swedish utopia *Kallocain*, by Karin Boye, members of the community are no longer called 'comrades', 'citizens', etc. They all have become 'fellow-soldiers'.

[153] Hall, G. R.: *The Black Fortnight, or the Invasion of 1915* (1904); Anon.: *A Time of Terror* (1906); Dawson, H. J.: *The Message* (1907); Sedgwick, S. N.: *The Last Persecution* (1909), etc., etc.

[154] Walker, J. B.: *America Fallen, the sequel to the European War* (1915); Wallace, Edgar: *1925, the Story of a Fatal Peace* (1915); Moffet, C.: *The Conquest of America* (1916).

[155] J.J.J.: *The Blue Shirts* (1926); Tweed, F. T.: *Blind Mouths* (1934); Frazer, S.: *A Shroud as Well as a Shirt* (1935); Balsdon, D.: *Sell England?* (1936); Watson, F.: *The Virgin King* (1937); Greenidge, T.: *Philip and the Dictator* (1938); Wells, H. G.: *The Holy Terror* (1939); Bishop, M.: *The Star Called Wormwood* (1941); O'Den, D.: *Crimson Courage* (1940); Alington, Adrian: *Sanity Island* (1941); Borodin, George: *Peace in Nobody's Time* (1944).

[156] Brown, D. and Serpell, C.: *Loss of Eden* (1940); Sackville-West, V.: *Grand Canyon* (1942); Hawkins, M.: *When Adolf Came* (1943).

[157] Shanks, Edward: *The People of the Ruins, a Story of the English Revolution and After* (1920); Graham, P. A.: *The Collapse of Homo Sapiens* (1923); Hamilton, Cicely: *Lest You Die* (1928); Gloag, John: *To-Morrow's Yesterday* (1932); Collier, John: *Tom's A-Cold* (1933); Llewellin, Alun: *The Strange Invaders* (1934); Mitchell, J. L.: *Gay Hunter* (1934); Macleod, J. G.: *Overture to Cambridge* (1936); Sheriff, R. C.: *The Hopkins Manuscript* (1939); Best, Herbert: *The Twenty-Fifth Hour* (1940); Stewart, G. R.: *Earth Abides* (1950); Gibbs, L.: *Late Final* (1951).

[158] Gloag, John: *To-Morrow's Yesterday*, p. 133.

[159] The invention of the atomic bomb at once produced corresponding forecasts: e.g. Rose, F. H.: *The Maniac's Dream, a Novel about the Atomic Bomb* (1946); Frank, P.: *Mr. Adam* (sterilization of all males) (1947); Kearney, C. B.: *The Great Calamity, an Atom Bomb Story* (1948).

[160] *1984*, p. 304.

[161] Graves, Robert: *Seven Days in New Crete* (1949), p. 41.

PART THREE, 1, *pages* 81–90

[162] This term has been employed by Chesterton in his introduction to *The Napoleon of Notting Hill*.

[163] Stapledon: *Last and First Men*, introduction.

[164] *Utopia*, p. 109.

[165] Wells, H. G.: *Experiment in Autobiography*, London 1934, vol. 1, p. 501.

[166] Jones, Henry Festing: *Samuel Butler, Author of Erewhon, a memoir*, 2 vols., London 1919, vol. 1, p. 156.

[167] Chesterton, G. K.: *Autobiography*, London 1936, p. 110.

[168] Haldane, Charlotte: *Truth Will Out*, London 1949, p. 15.

[169] Forster, E. M.: *Aspects of the Novel*, London 1927, p. 141.

[170] Plato: *Timaeus*, 19c, *Timaeus and Critias*, transl. by A. E. Taylor (1928).

[171] Eddy, W. A.: *Gulliver's Travels, a Critical Study*, Princeton 1923.

[172] *New Atlantis*, p. 350.

[173] A detailed study of terminological problems relating to imaginary voyages is provided by Ph. B. Gove in *The Imaginary Voyage in Prose Fiction 1700–1800*, Columbia Univ. Pr. 1941.

[174] Eddy, W. A.: *Gulliver's Travels*, p. 11.

[175] Read, Herbert: *English Prose Style*, London 1928, p. 146.

PART THREE, 2, *pages* 91–104

[176] Works of Lucian of Samosata, Oxford 1905, vol. 2, p. 137.

[177] Swift, J.: *Gulliver's Travels*, ed. by Herbert Davis, Oxford 1941, p. 275–6.

[178] Butler, S.: *Erewhon*, Shrewsbury edition 1923, vol. 2, p. 1.

[179] Wells, H. G.: *The Island of Dr. Moreau*, London 1896, p. 1.

[180] *Erewhon*, p. 1.

[181] e.g. Chesterton, G. K.: *The Napoleon of Notting Hill* and *The Flying Inn*; Macaulay, Rose: *Orphan Island* and *What Not*; Huxley, Aldous: *Brave New World* and *Ape and Essence*; Read, Herbert: *The Green Child*; Warner, Rex: *The Wild Goose Chase*; Orwell, George: *1984*, etc.

[182] Cantril: *Invasion from Mars*, p. 71.

[183] *Erewhon*, p. 242.

[184] Case, A. E.: *Four Essays on Gulliver's Travels*, Princeton 1945, p. 52.

[185] *Utopia*, p. 118.

[186] Bulwer-Lytton: *The Coming Race*, p. 8.

[187] *Erewhon*, p. 1.

[188] Godwin, Francis: *The Man in the Moon* (1638); Defoe, Daniel: *The*

Consolidator, or, Memoirs of Sundry Transactions from the World of the Moon (1705); Brunt, Samuel: *A Voyage to Cacklogallinia* (1727).

[189] Nicolson, Marjorie: *Voyages to the Moon*, New York 1948.

[190] Godwin, Francis: *The Man in the Moon* repr. in *Smith College Studies in Modern Languages*, vol. 19, Northampton, Mass. 1938, p. 18.

[191] Defoe, Daniel: *The Consolidator*, London 1705, p. 36.

[192] Lewis, C. S.: *Out of the Silent Planet*, p. 33.

[193] Wells, H. G.: *The Scientific Romances*, London 1933, p. vii–viii.

[194] Dupont, V.: *L'Utopie*, p. 717.

[195] Hudson, W. H.: *A Crystal Age*; Bellamy, E.: *Looking Backward*; Wells, H. G.: *The Sleeper Awakes*; Shanks, E.: *The People of the Ruins*, etc.

[196] Wells, H. G.: *Experiment in Autobiography*, vol. 1, p. 309.

[197] Stapledon, O.: *Last and First Men*; Meredith, E.: *Our Stranger*; Palmer, J.: *The Hesperides*, etc.

[198] Gloag, John: *To-Morrow's Yesterday.*

[199] Wells, H. G.: *The Scientific Romances*, p. vii–viii.

[200] Plato: *Timaeus*, 26 b.

[201] ibidem.

[202] *Utopia*, p. 116.

[203] Wells, H. G.: *The Time Machine*, p. 219–20.

[204] Meredith, E.: *Our Stranger, A Kinemato-Romance*, London 1936.

Part Three, 3, *pages* 105–112

[205] Lewis, C. S.: *Out of the Silent Planet*, p. 56–7.

[206] *Erewhon*, p. 5.

[207] Jones, H. F.: *Samuel Butler*, p. 151.

[208] Hudson, W. H.: *A Crystal Age* (1887), 2nd ed. 1906, p. 180.

[209] Todd, Ruthven: *Over the Mountain*, p. 5.

[210] ibidem., p. 8.

[211] Warner, Rex: *The Wild Goose Chase*, p. 1.

[212] Read, Herbert: *The Green Child*, 1935, p. 3.

[213] ibidem., p. 5.

[214] Todd, Ruthven: *The Lost Traveller* and *Over the Mountain.*

[215] *1984*, p. 80.

[216] *1984*, p. 299.

Part Three, 4, *pages* 113–119

[217] e.g. Benson, R. H.: *Dawn of All*; Onions, Oliver: *The New Moon*; Macleod, J. G.: *Overture to Cambridge*; Beresford, J. D.: *The Riddle of the Tower.*

[218] Lewis, C. S.: *Out of the Silent Planet*, p. 249.

[219] Wells, H. G.: *Modern Utopia*; *A Note to the Reader.*

[220] Treyer, H.: *Die Politische Insel* (1936).

[221] Forster, E. M.: *The Machine Stops* in *The Eternal Moment and Other Stories*, 1928, p. 1.

[222] Huxley, Aldous: *Ape and Essence* (1949), coll. ed., 1951, p. 82.

[223] ibidem, p. 85.

[224] ibidem, p. 87.

[225] Lewis, C. S.: *Out of the Silent Planet*, p. 252.

[226] Collier, John: *Tom's A-Cold* (1933), introduction.

[227] e.g. Benson, R. H.: *Lord of the World* (1907); Macaulay, Rose: *What Not* (1918); Haldane, Charlotte: *Man's World* (1926); Tillyard, Aelfrida: *Concrete* (1930); Huxley, Aldous: *Brave New World* (1932); Orwell, George: *1984* (1949).

[228] Huxley, Aldous: *Brave New World*, p. 1.

[229] *1984*, p. 5.

[230] Collier, John: *Tom's A-Cold*, p. 6.

[231] O'Neill, Joseph: *The Land Under England* (1935); Read, Herbert: *The Green Child* (1935); Warner, Rex: *The Wild Goose Chase* (1937).

PART THREE, 5, *pages* 120–132

[232] Liddell, Robert: *Treatise on the Novel*, London 1947, p. 55.

[233] Forster, E. M.: *Aspects of the Novel*, London 1927, p. 141.

[234] Leavis, F. R.: *The Great Tradition*, London 1948, p. 7.

[235] Ortega y Gasset: *Notes on the Novel*, Princeton 1948, p. 92.

[236] Myers, L. H.: *The Near and the Far*, London 1929, preface, p. 6.

[237] Huxley, Aldous: *Brave New World*, p. viii.

[238] *Erewhon*, p. xviii.

[239] *Brave New World*, p. 26.

[240] *Brave New World*, p. 18.

[241] *Brave New World*, p. vii.

[242] *Brave New World*, p. viii.

[243] *Brave New World*, p. ix.

[244] *Brave New World*, p. xi.

[245] Orwell, George: *Coming Up for Air*, London 1939, p. 183.

[246] ibidem, p. 183.

[247] ibidem, p. 203.

[248] ibidem, p. 202.

[249] *1984*, p. 83.

[250] *Modern Utopia*, Chapter 11, § 5.

[251] Plato: *Republic*, ix, 592.

[252] *Utopia*, p. 115.

[253] *Modern Utopia*, Chapter 11, § 5.

[254] see p. 3.

APPENDIX: AN ANNOTATED LIST OF ENGLISH UTOPIAN FANTASIES 1901-1951

The following list gives some idea of the range of modern utopian fantasy in English fiction. The list is mainly based on *The Times Literary Supplement*. Almost a hundred of the books listed have been studied, others merely glanced at. Those which did not seem to be promising in any way were not consulted. The list cannot claim to be complete. About a hundred sensational forecasts have been excluded from it, while quite a few lesser utopias may still be lurking among the fantasies listed in Everett E. Bleiler's *The Check-list of Fantastic Literature published in English*, Chicago, 1948. But it is unlikely that they would alter the picture of the utopian tradition.

1901 BUTLER, SAMUEL: *Erewhon*, revised ed.
" " *Erewhon Revisited.*

1902 KUPPARD, SKELTON (pseud.): *A Fortune from the Sky.* Miraculous science rules the world of the future.

PINKERTON, T.: *No Rates and Taxes, a Romance of Five Worlds.*

1903 STANLEY, WILLIAM: *The Case of the Fox, being the Prophecies under Hypnotism of the Period ending A.D. 1950, a Political Utopia.* A scientific world of international co-operation.

VAN LAUN, H.: *The Gates of Afree A.D. 1928.* A short romance of a new empire in Africa.

WILKIE, J.: *The Vision of Nehemiah Sintram.* Subterranean vision of a world where mammon rules.

1904 CHESTERTON, G. K.: *The Napoleon of Notting Hill.* Outburst of mediaevalism transforms England in the year 1984.

DICKBERRY, F.: *The Storm of London, a Social Rhapsody.* Dream of a return to simple life.

HALL, G. R.: *The Black Fortnight, or the Invasion of 1915.* One of the many invasions, ending with international federation.

ROLFE, FR. ('Baron Corvo'): *Hadrian the Seventh.* Englishman becomes Pope and reorganizes the world of the near future on Catholic lines.

TREVOR, PHILIP: *A Prince of the People, a Romance of Modern Royalty.* A Ruritanian satire on England, advocating a general reform of government.

1905 HARRIS-BURLAND, J. B.: *Dr. Silex.* Arctic expedition discovers a mediaeval society.

KERNAHAN, COULSON: *A World Without a Child.* England of the future, peopled by 'Pleasurists' and pessimists.

MIDDLETON, J. B.: *The God of this World.* Mammonism, the only religion, is overthrown and an international convention of peace and freedom takes place in 2036.

TURNER, REGINALD: *Peace on Earth.*

WELLS, H. G.: *A Modern Utopia.*

YOUNG, F. E.: *The War of the Sexes.* A future war has killed all the men of England except one.

1906 ANONYMOUS: *Star of the Morning, a Chronicle of Karyl the Great and the Revolt of 1920–22.* Equality of women.

DYVIRTA, TEMS (pseud.): *London's Transformation, a Suggestive Sketch of Days to Come.* Short scientific romance.

GRIFFITH, G.: *The Great Weather Syndicate.* A company exploits meteorological science and controls the world.

LEWIS, R. M.: *The Divine Gift.* A romance of human immortality.

REGNAS, C.: *The Land of Nison.* An immortal people who can do remarkable things by vital energy.

THORNE, GUY: *Made in His Image.* Slavery in England solves the problem of the unemployable.

WELLS, H. G.: *In the Days of the Comet.* Universal peace and social revival after catastrophe.

1907 ANONYMOUS: *What Might Have Been, the Story of a Social War.* Breakdown of a future socialist England.

BENSON, R. H.: *Lord of the World.* Materialist Religion of Mankind extinguishes Christianity.

BLATCHFORD, ROBERT: *The Sorcery Shop, an impossible Romance.* Socialist Arcadia on the lines of *News from Nowhere.*

BLYTH, JAMES: *The Tyranny.* Plutocratic England of the near future. People lose individualities in 'power room'.

BYATT, H.: *The Flight of Icarus.* England subdued by a 'King of the Jews.'

DAWSON, A. J.: *The Message.* England becomes a model nation, abolishes the party system, defeats Germany and sets up a German Republic.

MARTIN, J.: *The Immortal Light.* An antarctic expedition discovers a scientific utopia under the South Pole.

MOORE, FRANK F.: *The Marriage Lease.* Azalea, an English self-governing settlement, is run on strictly scientific principles. In the end religion triumphs over science.

NEWTE, HORACE W. C.: *The Master Beast, being the true account of the ruthless tyranny inflicted on the British people by Socialism A.D. 1888–2020.*

STRAUSS, RALPH: *The Dust which is God, an undimensional*

adventure. A short cosmic vision of three progressive worlds showing the evolution of the race towards perfection.

1908 COUTTS, TRISTRAM: *The Prodigal City*. Breakdown of State Socialism.

FLECKER, JAMES ELROY: *The Last Generation, a story of the future*. In Collected Prose, London 1922. Extreme materialism results in death of mankind.

KOEBEL, W. H.: *The Singular Republic*. Romance in Neuvonie, a facile eutopia.

MAYNE, J. D.: *The Triumph of Socialism, and How It Succeeded*. Shows the disastrous results of the great Socialist Triumph at the elections of 1912.

NAVARCHUS (pseud.): *The World's Awakening*. A future global war.

REETH, ALLAN: *Legions of the Dawn*. Matriarchy in the interior of Africa.

WELLS, H. G.: *The War in the Air*. Collapse of civilization as a result of universal aerial fighting.

WILSON, JESSE: *When the Women Reign 1930*. Anti-feminist fantasy.

1909 ANONYMOUS: *Red England, a Tale of Socialist Terror*.

BARLOW, JAMES WILLIAM: *The Immortals' Great Quest*. Immortal race on Venus striving for ever greater knowledge of the origin of universe and on the destiny of mankind.

CASSIUS MINOR (pseud.): *The Finding of Mercia*. Puritan simple life utopia on an unknown island.

CLYDE, IRENE: *Beatrice the Sixteenth*. Describes the sexless country Armeria.

EVERETT, FRANCES: *John Bull: Socialist*. A picture of England after 30 years of socialist rule.

FOX-DAVIES, A. C.: *The Sex Triumphant*. Anti-feminist fantasy.

KIPLING, RUDYARD: *With the Night Mail, a Story of 2000 A.D*. Short story picturing the achievements of a scientific civilization.

RICHARDS, CHARLES NAPIER: *Atalanta, or, Twelve Months in the Evening Star*. Social, religious, and amorous experiences on Venus, whose inhabitants are far in advance of us.

SEDGWICK, S. N.: *The Last Persecution*. In 1947 Europe is under the sway of the yellow races and Christianity is cruelly persecuted.

1910 ANONYMOUS: *The Next Crusade, a Cautionary Political Story*. Satirical forecast, attacking all kinds of political abuses.

ANONYMOUS: *An Amazing Revolution and After*. A vast confederacy establish a 'sane Socialism' all over the world.

ASHBEE, C. R.: *The Building of Thelema*. A utopian romance based on Morris's gospel of beauty, craftsmanship, and comradeship.

HERBERT, E. G.: *Newaera, a Socialist Romance*. Anti-socialist.

1910 LE QUEUX, WILLIAM: *The Unkown To-Morrow, How the Rich Fared at the Hands of the Poor, together with a full account of the Social Revolution in England.* Sensational anti-socialist tale.

PRINCE, EDWARD: *Wake Up, England, Being the Amazing Story of John Bull: Socialist.* Illustrates the perils of socialism.

WELLS, H. G.: *The Sleeper Awakes.* (Revised ed. of *When the Sleeper Wakes*, 1899). Describes nightmarish plutocracy of the future and the revolt against it.

1911 ANONYMOUS: *The Laws of Leflo.* Arcadian anarchy in the middle of an African desert is proved to be a dismal failure.

BENSON, R. H.: *Dawn of All.* Vision of a future world turned Catholic. Science and religion are reconciled. Heretics are persecuted.

MINNETT, CORA: *The Day After To-Morrow.* In 1975 aviation has become universal, America is a monarchy, and immense benefits have followed the universal equality of women.

1912 HODGSON, WILLIAM HOPE: *The Night Land.* Nightmare vision of an age to come. The last millions of humanity are gathered in a colossal pyramid surrounded by ghoulish horrors.

HOLT-WHITE, W.: *The World Stood Still.* Multimillionaires controlling the world resign. Chaos results. So they kindly take over again.

HOUSMAN, LAURENCE: *John of Jingalo, the Story of a Monarch in Difficulties.* Able Ruritanian satire, mainly concerned with the equality of women.

KIPLING, RUDYARD: *As Easy as A.B.C.* Future world dominated by technocratic Aerial Board of Control, the A.B.C.

1913 MAWSON, L. A.: *Methods from Mars.* A Martian visitor tells the author about a Martian utopia.

PETWORTH, ALGERNON: *The Little Wicket Gate.* Describes a human race in perfect accord with nature, art, machinery, and the fundamentals of religion.

1914 CARRELL, F.: *2010.* Poverty and disease are annihilated, science rules, even men's minds can be changed by a new invention.

CHESTERTON, G. K.: *The Flying Inn.* Joyless Mahommedan supremacy in England of uncertain date. All inns are suppressed.

GUBBINS, H.: *The Elixir of Life, or, 2905 A.D.* Scientific achievements of a future generation.

HOUSMAN, LAURENCE: *The Royal Runaway, and Jingalo in Revolt.* Continues *John of Jingalo* (1912).

WELLS, H. G.: *The World Set Free.* Reconstruction on collectivistic lines after an atomic war.

1915 GROGAN, G.: *A Drop in Infinity.* Hero discovers a grand underground world; on his return to the upper world he founds a new community.

MARSHALL, ARCHIBALD: *Upsidonia.* An Erewhonian satire: the poor are the aristocracy, the rich are ashamed of their wealth.

1915 WALLACE, EDGAR: *1925, the Story of a Fatal Peace*. Disastrous results of unfounded trust in Germany's good faith.

1916 MOFFETT, CLEVELAND: *The Conquest of America, a Romance of Disaster and Victory U.S.A. 1921*. A forecast of America's fate after the defeat of England.

VAUGHAN, H. M.: *Meleager*. Meleager is a small planet where a hierarchical utopia reigns.

1917 GERARD, MORICE: *The New Order*. England's religious reform after the war.

1918 BERESFORD, LESLIE: *The Kingdom of Content*. After a fight between trusts, people finally find content on the ruins of London.

GREGORY, OWEN: *Meccania, the Super State*. A mechanical and material state government, carried to its extreme logical development in 1970.

MACAULAY, ROSE: *What Not, a prophetic Comedy*. England of the near future. 'Ministry of Brains' passes Mental Progress Act and Mind Training Bill in order to improve the race.

ONIONS, OLIVER: *The New Moon, a Romance of Reconstruction*. The war is over, England is reconstructed on the lines of More's *Utopia*. People are badged, numbered, and graded.

ROUSSEAU, VICTOR: *The Apostle of the Cylinder*. An extreme scientific materialist is transported to a future world. He finds a materialistic society based on pure reason. Wells has become The Prophet.

1919 COLWYN, JOHN: *A City Without a Church*. Social revolution in 1938, but the need of religion asserts itself.

HAGGARD, RIDER: *When the World Shook*. On a small island the 'Sons of Wisdom' had discovered all the mechanical knowledge long ago, but were defeated by barbarism. Satirical allegory.

NEWTE, HORACE W. C.: *The Red Fury, Britain under Bolshevism*.

SHARP, EVELYN: *Somewhere in Christendom*. World dominated by Bolshevism.

BRAMAH, ERNEST: *The Secret of the League, the Story of a Social War*.

1920 HAMBROOK, EMERSON C.: *The Red To-Morrow*. Britain under Bolshevism.

PALLEN, C. B.: *Crucible Island, a Romance, an Adventure, and an Experiment*. Picture of a socialist utopia which proves a dismal failure.

SHANKS, EDWARD: *The People of the Ruins, a Story of the English Revolution and After*. General strike in 1924 marks the beginning of the collapse of civilization. 150 years later England is reduced to neolithical barbarism.

UNITAS (pseud.): *The Dream City*. Describes Delectaland, a facile socialist anarchy.

1921 BERESFORD, J. D.: *Revolution*. Story of a social upheaval in England of the near future.

1921 BERESFORD, LESLIE: *The Great Image.* A hundred years later science has progressed immensely, but utopia is not yet realized. Humanity will always be groping for the ideal, without ever attaining it.

NEDRAM (pseud.): *John Sagur.* Scientist becomes master of the world. His absolutism produces happiness and prosperity.

ROSS, CHARLES: *The Fly-By-Nights.* England of the Future under prohibition.

GRIFFITHS, ISABEL: *Three Worlds.* Earth, Jupiter, and Mars. On Jupiter a kind of earthly paradise has been realized, Mars is even worse than our planet.

1922 SCRYMSOUR, ELLA: *The Perfect World, a romance of strange people and strange places.*

1923 ANONYMOUS: *When Woman Rules! A Tale of the First Women's Government.* Failure of feminism.

CAMPBELL, DUNCAN: *The Last Millionaire, a Tale of the Old World and the New.* In 1959 the Labour Party triumphs and nationalizes the vital industries.

GRAHAM, P. ANDERSON: *The Collapse of Homo Sapiens.* Wars have destroyed civilization. The few survivors live in the woods and cannot believe that scientific and mechanical aids ever existed.

GUNPAT (pseud.): *Harilek, a Romance of Modern Central Asia.* Arcadian utopia realized in Gobi desert.

KNOX, RONALD A.: *Memories of the Future: Being Memoirs of the Years 1915–1972, written in the Year of Grace 1988 by Opal, Lady Porstock.* Satirical forecast demonstrating that the idea of progress is an illusion.

NICHOLS, ROBERT: *Golgatha and Co.* (in 'Fantastica'). The plutocratic 'Brains of Power' control the world. They cleverly exploit Christianity to keep the people quiet. An enormous pseudo-religious propaganda campaign is launched.

ODLE, E. V.: *The Clockwork Man.* The clockwork man is a kind of time machine and provides a good deal of evolutionary instruction.

WELLS, H. G.: *Men Like Gods.* These wonderful men of the future live in arcadian simplicity. All social problems having been solved, they find an outlet for their energies in scientific research.

1924 LYNCH, ARTHUR: *Seraph Wings.* The hero becomes the autocratic ruler of England and establishes a social utopia. Westminster Abbey, the last trace of feudalism, is removed.

MACAULAY, ROSE: *Orphan Island.* A ship full of children founders on an unknown island in the Pacific. Due to the influence of the governess the emerging society is replete with the most absurd Victorian taboos and class distinctions.

MACCLURE, VICTOR: *Ultimatum, a Romance of the Air.* A New League of Nations, ruled by a scientist, dominates the world.

WELLS, H. G.: *The Dream.* A member of a future utopian generation has a particularly vivid dream about the life of the past. He tells this dream to his comrades and is interrupted by utopian comments.

1925 CORON, HANNAH: *Ten Years Hence?* Disastrous results of Labour policy.

RICHARDSON, E.: *Newtopia.*

WRIGHT, S. FOWLER: *The Amphibians: a Romance of 500,000 Years Hence.* Evolutionary fantasy, portraying supermen.

1926 DESMOND, SHAW: *Ragnarok.* War in the air plus chemicals destroy civilization.

GEORGE, W. L.: *Children of the Morning.* After a shipwreck a boat containing some 70 children drifts to a tropical island. The book depicts the growth of social institutions from an imaginary state of innocence.

HALDANE, CHARLOTTE: *Man's World.* This Brave New World has been purged of all retrograde persons by a devastating chemical war. The direction of affairs is in the hand of scientists and geneticists. Philosophers and politicians have been eliminated. A lonely artist who tries to rediscover religious values finally commits suicide.

J.J.J.: *The Blue Shirts.* British Fascist organization of the future.

JACOMB, C. E.: *And a New Earth.* An island utopia, peopled first entirely by children. A matriarchal organization emerges, combined with an astounding scientific apparatus.

JAEGER, M.: *The Question Mark.* After a two hundred years' cataleptic trance a bank-clerk wakes up to find a new and radiant England. Wealth is now general and the social organization is perfect. The old class distinctions have been abolished, now there are only the 'intellectuals' and the 'normals'.

O'DUFFY, EIMAR: *King Goshawk and the Birds.* Some 50 years hence Cuchulain defeats King Goshawk, the most powerful ruler of the new plutocratic kingdoms, who wants to remove the remaining sources of joy from this earth.

POWELL, GERALD: *All Things New.* Scientist ends all wars.

RIDLEY, F. H.: *The Green Machine.* On Mars; the ants, who are very clever beasts in mathematics and social science, dominate degenerated man.

SPANNER, E. E.: *The Broken Trident.* England surrenders to a powerful, but benevolent Germany and universal peace sets in.

1927 CHESTERTON, G. K.: *The Return of Don Quixote.* Describes another outburst of English mediaevalism.

LEGGE, J. G.: *The Millennium.* A satire on scientific reformers.

MARGRIE, W.: *The Story of a Great Experiment. How England Produced the First Superman.*

MONTAGUE, C. E.: *Right Off the Map.* A satirical attack on England by means of a corrupt imaginary country which is defeated by an efficient enemy and consequently loses its independent existence.

1927 OLLIVANT, ALFRED: *Tomorrow*. A strictly organized utopian England controlled by a central authority with absolute powers. By a cult of physical health and mystical science the superman is slowly evolved.

1928 CALLAGHAN, STELLA: *Nor Shall My Sword Sleep*. An extremely rich young industrialist founds a utopian model colony for his workers.

DUDLEY, EUSTACE: *The Challenge, a Story of Conspiracy and the Coming Crash*. About 1935 a Socialist Dictator of England turns Catholic and makes Europe Catholic, happy, and prosperous.

FORSTER, E. M.: *The Machine Stops* (in 'The Eternal Moment and other Stories'). Machinery controls the world, the individuals live underground and are almost completely isolated. The son who wants to see his mother is a freak. Finally the vast machinery breaks down, a new, more natural life begins again on the surface of the earth.

GRIERSON, FRANCIS D.: *Heart of the Moon*. Inside the moon everything is state-controlled. No one is hungry or unemployed, but everybody is subjected to the oppressive central authority.

HAMILTON, CICELY: *Lest Ye Die*. Imaginary war causes relapse into barbarism. Towns and roads have disappeared. The few survivors settle in the woods and are perpetually afraid of one another.

O'DUFFY, EIMAR: *The Spacious Adventures of the Man in the Street*. An amusing paradoxical utopia on a distant star. The utopians are partly moral paragons, partly satirically inverted human beings.

WELLS, H. G.: *Mr. Blettsworthy on Rampole Island*. The hero is the 'Sacred Lunatic' among a kind of yahoos.

WINCH, E.: *The Mountain of Gold*. An unknown Brazilian tribe practises a refined arcadian communism.

1929 BOWHAY, B. L.: *Elenchus Brown, the Story of an Experimental Utopia*. A small colony on an island try out different social systems. None of them proves satisfactory.

GUEST, ERNEST: *At the End of the World, a Vision*. History of the world from 10,000 A.D. till human life ends. First, a future world state is directed by the 'men of minds'. All personal desires are subordinated to social obligation. Slowly the doom of mankind draws near. When the last man is dead it looks as if a huge joke has been played on humanity.

MITCHISON, NAOMI: *Cardiff A.D. 1935* (in 'Barbarian Stories'). Human sacrifice has been reintroduced. Once a year there is a ceremonial drowning of a capitalist in order to appease the poor.

WRIGHT, S. FOWLER: *The World Below*. A forecast of the far future; a kind of superman has evolved.

1930 JERROLD, DOUGLAS: *Storm over Europe*. In the imaginary country of Cisalpina the conflict between secular utopianism and the ideal of the Civitas Dei is enacted. Utopianism is defeated.

1930 MILES (pseud.): *The Seventh Bowl.* The elixir of life is invented and all the babies are killed. In 1990 the earthly paradise is ruled by an all-seeing bureaucracy.

STAPLEDON, W. OLAF: *Last and First Men, a Story of the Near and Far Future.*

SUTHERLAND, JAMES: *The Narrative of Jasper Weeple, Being an Account of his Strange Journey to the Land of Midanglia.* Midanglia is a mediaeval utopia.

TILLYARD, AELFRIDA: *Concrete, a Story of Two Hundred Years Hence.* Strictly regimented utopia based on extreme scientific materialism. People volunteer for euthanasia from sheer boredom. Heroine escapes to a tropical island where Christianity is still a living force.

WELLS, H. G.: *The Autocracy of Mr. Parham.* A Master Spirit from Mars enters Mr. Parham. He becomes Lord Paramount of England and dismisses Parliament. War between America and England ensues, but in the end it is all a dream.

1931 CHILTON, H. H.: *The Lost Children.* Inside a mountain some travellers discover the country where thc Pied Piper has led the children of Hamelin. Their descendants have made a utopian life for themselves.

NEWMAN, BERNARD: *Armoured Doves.* A 'League of Scientists' prevents all wars by utopian science.

HETT, JOHN: *Our Glorious Future.* Science and religion are reconciled; party politics, unemployment, and war are abolished. All this as a result of messages transmitted by a miracle child.

1932 FREESE, STANLEY: *The Ten Year Plan, a Dream of 1940.* Mostly concerned with town-planning.

GLOAG, JOHN: *To-Morrow's Yesterday.* A.D. 3,000,000 catmen watch a play with scenes in 1933, 1968, 1993, 2300, and 12000. The gradual relapse into barbarism is described. Later the cat-race rises to rationality by abolishing sex.

HUXLEY, ALDOUS: *Brave New World.*

JAMES, ROWLAND: *While England Slept.* Miraculous revival of religious life all over England.

STAPLEDON, W. OLAF: *Last Men in London.* Again describes some of the Last Men of *Last and First Men* (1930).

WRIGHT, S. FOWLER: *The New Gods Lead.* Short stories directed against scientific utopianism.

VINES, SHERARD: *Return, Belphegor!* A fantastic tale of a religious Fundamentalist revival in the England of the near future.

1933 ARLEN, MICHAEL: *Man's Mortality.* International Aircraft and Airways, Inc. control the world. Democracy is abolished.

COLLIER, JOHN: *Tom's A-Cold.* Before the year 2000 England has slipped back into barbarism. Old superstitions and taboos re-emerge. Different settlements take various lines towards the development of a new civilization.

1933 DEARMER, GEOFFREY: *Saint on Holiday*. The 'Ministry of Grace' has gradually mastered public opinion and rules by means of an enormous organization.

O'DUFFY, EIMAR: *Asses in Clover*. Satirical picture of a future plutocracy.

STUART, FRANCIS: *Glory*. Violent intrigue in a world controlled by the Trans-Continental Aero-Routes.

WELLS, H. G.: *The Shape of Things to Come, the Ultimate Revolution*. Utopian reconstruction after a colossal war.

WRIGHT, S. FOWLER: *Power*. The hero becomes dictator of England and abolishes debt-collecting, vivisection, and birth-control.

1934 CURTIS, MONICA: *Landslide*. Western Europe under a dictator who establishes cruel discipline in the name of Confederal Glory. Democrats are sent to torture camps.

GLOAG, JOHN: *Winter's Youth*. Scientific rejuvenation in a world grown peaceful because all the powers had the atomic bomb.

LLEWELLIN, ALUN: *The Strange Invaders*. Long after a future destructive war a decadent communist city is invaded by robots.

MITCHELL, J. LESLIE: *Gay Hunter*. The revolt of the submen against the hierarchs has destroyed civilization. Some fascists of the far future want to reindustrialize Britain, but are blown to pieces.

MOSELEY, MABOTH: *War upon Women*. An attack on dictatorship in an imaginary country.

PALMER, JOHN LESLIE: *One Sane Man*. One man can control the weather and plans a general political reform, but is defeated by conservative stupidity.

REID, LESLIE: *Cauldron Bubble*. Extreme nationalism produces a destructive war in some imaginary countries.

TWEED, T. F.: *Blind Mouths*. Materialist dictatorship in the huge country of Danubia. Christianity is suppressed.

1935 CROSS, VICTORIA (pseud.): *Martha Brown, M.P., a Girl of To-Morrow*. Matriarchy in the thirtieth century.

FRAZER, SHAMUS: *A Shroud as Well as a Shirt*. Describes a future Fascist England.

GUESSWELL, ELSIE K. (pseud.): *When Yvonne Was Dictator*. Woman's complete equality is established.

LANCING, GEORGE: *Fraudulent Conversion, a Romance of the Gold Standard*. A professor, completely ignorant of economics, starts social reform and is attacked on all sides. After a long struggle he converts the most powerful men and England is on the point of becoming a utopia.

O'NEILL, JOSEPH: *The Land Under England*. Describes a totalitarian utopia where the little individual emotions are absorbed by the love for the common good. There are only two classes: the leaders and the robotlike citizens, whose minds have been 'rearranged'.

1935 READ, HERBERT: *The Green Child.* Contrasts a primitive worldly utopia in South America and a spiritual one under England.

WRIGHT, S. FOWLER: *Prelude in Prague, a Story of the War of 1938.* Describes how the Nazis annex Czechoslovakia.

1936 BALSDON, DACRE: *Sell England?* In about a thousand years most of the English have emigrated to Africa where they live under a totalitarian régime. In England itself a small and extremely decadent aristocracy has survived.

BERTRAM, ANTHONY: *The King Sees Red.* A utopian satire on Fascism.

MACLEOD, JOSEPH GORDON: *Overture to Cambridge, a Satirical Story.* A nightmare of the future describing a world inhabited by Blues, Yellows, and other colour-mad nations, who destroy each other by everlasting war. Finally civilization collapses and a new primitivism reigns.

MEREDITH, EDGAR: *Our Stranger, a Kinemato-Romance.* In 1971 the social millennium has set in and the spiritual evolution of man is influenced by the people of the far future.

O'NEILL, JOSEPH: *Day of Wrath.* A terrible future war destroys civilization.

PALMER, JOHN: *The Hesperides, a Looking-Glass Fugue.* Hesperus is the planet where the completely rational totalitarian world-state is established. The community is everything, the individual is nothing.

PHILLPOTTS, EDEN: *The Owl of Athene.* Mankind combines against a common enemy and achieves a new order.

SMITH, WAYLAND: *The Machine Stops.* A scientific fantasy depicting the dawn of a super-civilization.

STEVENSON, D. E.: *The Empty World, a Romance of the Future.* A small colony survives a future catastrophe and is organized on eugenic principles.

TUNSTALL, W. C. BRIAN: *Eagles Restrained.* The International Air Police of the League of Nations controls the world.

1937 SHIEL, M. P.: *The Young Men Are Coming.* A combination of social reform and scientific fantasy concerned with youth-medicine.

STAPLEDON, OLAF: *Star-Maker.* An evolutionary fantasy ranging over billions of years.

WARNER, REX: *The Wild Goose Chase.* A symbolical journey to a totalitarian utopia where extreme scientific materialism has succeeded in perverting all traditional human values.

WATSON, FRANCIS: *The Virgin King.* A utopian satire on the evils of Fascism.

WELLS, H. G.: *Star Begotten.* The Martians, who are vastly superior to mankind, exert a beneficial influence on humanity.

1938 CLOUSTON, J. STORER: *Not Since Genesis.* England solves the world's problems by a lucky political coup.

1938 DESMOND, SHAW: *Chaos.* Incessant chaotic war of the future.

GREENIDGE, TERENCE: *Philip and the Dictator.* Satire on Fascism.

LAMB, WILLIAM: *The World Ends.* A natural catastrophe produces another patriarchal age.

LEWIS, C. S.: *Out of the Silent Planet.* An allegorical satire on scientific materialism by means of a spiritual utopia on Mars where the inhabitants are in living contact with the deity.

LINKLATER, ERIC: *The Impregnable Women.* A future war is cut short because all the women go on love-strike.

MARVELL, ANDREW: *Minimum Man.* The Lilliputian minimum men succeed in abolishing a totalitarian régime in the England of the future.

TODD, RUTHVEN: *Over the Mountain.* A symbolical journey to a nightmare country ruled by secret police.

WRIGHT, S. FOWLER: *The Adventure of Wyndham Smith.* A few thousand years hence a scientific utopia is realized and the machines do all the work. The result is frustration.

1939 HAMILTON, PATRICK: *Impromptu in Moribundia.* A satirical utopia describing a kind of inverted England on another planet.

MACOWAN, NORMAN: *Glorious Morning.* Religious revival in a country where the state is everything.

MARVEL, ANDREW: *Three Men Make a World.* After an immensely destructive war the four remaining millions in England establish a primitive peasant community.

PARKINSON, H. F.: *They Shall Not Die.* One third of the population can be made immortal, but at the age of 150 the soul leaves the body in a fit of mania.

SHERIFF, R. C.: *The Hopkins Manuscript.* A world war destroys civilization.

WELLS, H. G.: *The Holy Terror.* The story of Rud Whitlow, a dictator, who brings about the coming of the world state. After Whitlow's death eutopia is established.

1940 BEST, HERBERT: *The Twenty-Fifth Hour.* After the annihilation of mankind the Nile valley becomes the cradle of a new civilization. The new community is ruled by a philosopher-king, and possession is held in contempt.

BROWN, DOUGLAS (and SERPELL, C.): *Loss of Eden.* A detailed picture of England under Nazi rule.

GLOAG, JOHN: *Manna.* A satirical utopian fantasy about an edible fungus that brings contentment and therefore is abolished.

NOYES, ALFRED: *The Last Man.* After the breakdown of humanity a small religious congregation sets itself the task of recreating human society.

O'DEN, DANIEL: *Crimson Courage.* A nightmare of a dictator-ridden country where all initiative is crushed.

1941 ALINGTON, ADRIAN: *Sanity Island.* Satirical utopia directed against communists and Nazis.

1941 BERESFORD, J. D.: *What Dreams May Come . . .* A dream of a utopia in a future non-mechanical age. Man has undergone biological changes and every member of the community slowly ascends the ladder of a spiritual hierarchy.

BISHOP, MORCHARD: *The Star Called Wormwood.* A fantasy of the future conceived as a satire on the second world war.

1942 BERESFORD, J. D.: *A Common Enemy.* A world-wide natural catastrophe forces mankind to social reconstruction on new and better lines.

JAMESON, STORM: *Then We Shall Hear Singing.* A victorious race starts scientific experiments on the conquered, but memory, which is in danger of being eliminated, proves indestructible.

SACKVILLE-WEST, V.: *Grand Canyon.* Describes the invasion of the U.S.A. after the defeat of Britain.

SAMUEL, H. L. (Viscount Samuel): *An Unkown Land.* A scientific, but liberal utopia on an island in the Pacific, Bacon's New Atlantis. The system of government consists in general good will. This in its turn is based on a superior intelligence, which has been achieved by enlarging the human brain.

STAPLEDON, OLAF: *The Darkness and the Light.* Two possible courses of future development are opposed to each other. On the one hand there is destruction and darkness, on the other spiritual rebirth and light. Both imaginary histories are presented in detail.

VANSITTART, PETER: *I am the World.* Describes the rise and fall of a prodigious dictator in a small imaginary country.

1943 ALLAN, MEA: *Change of Heart.* The second world war is over, but peace is endangered by the revival of Nazism, which threatens the established unity of Europe.

HAWKINS, MARTIN: *When Adolf Came.* The Germans conquer England, but fail to abolish English traditions. In the end they are defeated by the underground movement.

KEARNEY, CHALMERS: *Erone.* Utopia on Uranus where man's spiritual outlook has been changed and the economic structure of society is based on modified communism.

1944 ASKHAM, FRANCIS: *The Heart Consumed.* Describes a future training centre where the prospective leaders of the twenty-first century are educated.

BERESFORD, J. D. (and WYNNE-TYSON, E.): *The Riddle of the Tower.* Mankind descends through successful regimentation and mechanization to the final status of insects.

BORODIN, GEORGE: *Peace in Nobody's Time.* A utopian satire on dictatorship.

KING-HALL, LOU: *Fly Envious Time.* In 1979 the Federal Union of Democracy has been established for some time and women have achieved complete equality with men.

TODD, RUTHVEN: *The Lost Traveller.* A surrealist fantasy describing a city in the desert where the individual has lost his rights.

1945 LEWIS, C. S.: *That Hideous Strength, a Modern Fairy Tale for Grown-Ups.* Some time after the second world war the Satanic powers work through the National Institute for Co-ordinated Experiments, which combines inhuman science with state despotism.

ORWELL, GEORGE: *Animal Farm.* A satirical beast-utopia tracing the rise and fall of communist ideals.

1946 BAKER, GORDON: *None So Blind.* The re-education of the Germans in the principles of democracy and humanism during the next thirty years.

HANLEY, JAMES: *What Farrar Saw.* Points out how future mechanization defeats its own ends.

MOTTRAM, R. H.: *Visit of the Princess, a Romance of the 1960's.* A regimented Britain of the future and its reactions to the visit of a princess from an unknown island.

ROSE, F. H.: *The Maniac's Dream, a Novel about the Atomic Bomb.* The future development of atomic energy, which is exploited by a band of inhuman scientists.

1947 DE CHAIR, SOMERSET: *The Teetotalitarian State.* A satirical prophecy mainly concerned with contemporary politics.

FRANK, PAT: *Mr. Adam.* An atomic bomb fantasy.

GREEN, F. L.: *A Fragment of Glass.* A comic strip in a newspaper becomes a world-wide moral influence. After producing a change of government it also changes all human life.

NOTT, KATHLEEN: *The Dry Deluge.* A brilliant scientist founds an underground community whose purpose is to become immortal.

VENNING, HUGH: *The End, a Projection, not a Prophecy.* Britain a hundred years hence under the influence of a man who calls himself the head of the 'Greater Roman Empire' and claims power over the world.

1948 COLVIN, IAN: *Domesday Village.* A satirical fantasy about a totally regimented, bureaucratized, and standardized England of the future. A small village has hitherto escaped the notice of the officials, but is soon incorporated into the system.

HEARD, GERALD: *Doppelgangers.* Describes an episode from the Psychological Revolution in 1997. Earth is dominated by a benevolent dictator who uses popular science to keep everybody happy.

KEARNEY, C. B.: *The Great Calamity.* An atomic bomb catastrophe produces a religious revival.

LISTER, STEPHEN: *Hail Bolonia!* An island in the South Atlantic is ruled with enlightened Christian simplicity.

1949 GRAVES, ROBERT: *Seven Days in New Crete.* A forecast of an arcadian hierarchy based on a new interpretation of magic and sex. In the end the conception of life is deepened by the reintroduction of evil.

HUXLEY, ALDOUS: *Ape and Essence.* After a comprehensive atomic bomb catastrophe, man undergoes biological changes.

1949 Love is extinct, only collective seasonal sexual intercourse remains. The place of traditional religion has been taken by a hysterical worship of Belial, the god of evil.

ORWELL, GEORGE: *1984*.

1950 CAPON, PAUL: *The Other Side of the Sun*. Utopian life on the planet Antigeos. Society has developed from matriarchy to sexual freedom. Social classes are abolished. Because economy is planned, work is reduced to the absolute minimum.

STEWART, GEORGE R.: *Earth Abides*. The population of a future age has been mysteriously reduced and lives under primeval conditions.

1951 DUNSANY, LORD: *The Last Revolution*. Revolt of robots.

GIBBS, LEWIS: *Late Final*. In 1960 an Englishman comes back from a concentration camp in Siberia to a devastated England.

GUERARD, J. A.: *Night Journey*. A decaying future world exhausted by endless pointless wars.

MATTHEWS, RONALD: *Red Sky at Night*. A miraculous crusade causes the collapse of the Soviet system. The world turns Roman Catholic and peace is established.

WEST, ANTHONY: *Another Kind*. A future war in which Britain becomes the battleground for American and Russian tanks.

BIBLIOGRAPHY

The study of utopias involves the study of the history of civilization. Therefore it is hardly possible to make an adequate selection of works dealing with all the subjects related to utopian thought. The reader who is interested in the social and cultural background of modern utopian fiction is referred to the excellent bibliography contained in Karl Mannheim's *Man and Society in an Age of Reconstruction, Studies in Modern Social Structure*, London 1940.

Trying to list all the works on individual utopias and authors would also lead beyond the range of this study. The following list only takes into account books and articles that are either concerned with the principles of utopian creation or with a series of utopias, or with both.

ATKINSON, GEOFFREY: *Les Relations des Voyages du 17ème siècle et l'évolution des idées*. Paris 1926.

BERNERI, MARIE-LOUISE: *Journey Through Utopia*. London 1951.

BLOOMFIELD, PAUL: *Imaginary Worlds*. London 1932.

BLÜHER, RUDOLF: *Moderne Utopien, ein Beitrag zur Geschichte des Sozialismus*. Leipzig 1920.

BRASCH, MORITZ: *Sozialistische Phantasiestaaten* (in *Gesammelte Essays zur Neueren Philologie und Literatur*, pp. 57–125). Leipzig 1887.

BRUEGGEMANN, FRITZ: *Utopie und Robinsonade* (Forschungen zur Neueren Literaturgeschichte, vol. xlvi). Weimar 1914.

CHILD, H. H.: *Some English Utopias* (Publications of the Royal Society of Literature of the United Kingdom, pp. 31–60). London 1933.

COATES, J. B.: *Ten Modern Prophets* (On Gerald Heard, Aldous Huxley, Olaf Stapledon, H. G. Wells). London 1944.

DOREN, ALFRED: *Wunschräume und Wunschzeiten*. Leipzig 1927.

DUPONT, V.: *L'utopie et le roman utopique dans la littérature anglaise*. Paris 1941.

GOVE, PH. B.: *The Imaginary Voyage in Prose Fiction 1700–1800*. New York 1941.

HAHN, A.: *Grenzenloser Optimismus, die biologischen und technischen Möglichkeiten der Menschheit. Utopiologie*. Prag 1939.

HERTZLER, J. O.: *The History of Utopian Thought*. London 1922.

HIPPEL, O. VON: *Die pädagogische Dorf-Utopie der Aufklärung*. Langensalza 1939.

KAUFMANN, MORITZ: *Utopias; or, schemes of social improvement, from Sir Thomas More to Karl Marx*. London 1879.

KLEINWAECHTER, FRIEDRICH: *Die Staatsromane*. Wien 1891.

KIRCHENHEIM, A. VON: *Schlaraffia Politica, Geschichte der Dichtungen vom besten Staate*. Leipzig 1892.

MANNHEIM, KARL: *Ideology and Utopia, an Introduction to the Sociology of Knowledge*. London 1936.

MASSÒ, GILDO: *Education in Utopias*. New York 1927.

MOHL, ROBERT VON: *Die Staatsromane* (in *Die Geschichte und Literatur der Staatswissenschaften*, III, pp. 167–214). Erlangen 1855.

MUELLER, W. D.: *Geschichte der Utopia-Romane der Weltliteratur*. Bochum 1938.

MUMFORD, LEWIS: *The Story of Utopias, Ideal Commonwealths and Social Myths*. London 1923.

NEWBOLT, HENRY: *A Modern Utopia* (in Studies in Green and Grey, pp. 102–34). London 1926.

NICOLSON, MARJORIE: *Voyages to the Moon*. New York 1948.

PARRINGTON, VERNON LOUIS JR.: *American Dreams, a Study of American Utopias*. Brown University 1947.

PATCH, HOWARD ROLLIN: *The Other World according to descriptions in Medieval Literature*. Cambridge, Mass. 1950.

PRYS, J.: *Der Staatsroman des 16. und 17. Jahrhunderts*. Würzburg 1916.

ROHDE, ERWIN: *Der griechische Roman und seine Vorläufer*. Leipzig 1900.

ROSS, HARRY: *Utopias Old and New*. London 1938.

RUSSELL, F. T.: *Touring Utopia*. New York 1932.

SIMON, WOLFGANG: *Die englische Utopie im Lichte der Entwicklungslehre*. Diss. Breslau 1937.

STAMMLER, RUDOLF: *Utopien*. Deutsche Rundschau, Bd. 70, 1892.

TREYER, HANS: *Das Problem der Utopie*. Deutsche Rundschau, Bd. 183, 1920.

TREYER, HANS: *Die politische Insel, Eine Geschichte der Utopien von Platon bis zur Gegenwart*. Leipzig 1936.

TUVESON, ERNEST LEE: *Millennium and Utopia, a study in the Background of the Idea of Progress* (seventeenth-century philosophy). Los Angeles 1949.

VOIGT, ANDREAS: *Die sozialen Utopien*. Leipzig 1906.

INDEX